# HOW TO DINE IN STYLE

# HOW TO DINE IN STYLE

## THE ART OF ENTERTAINING, 1920

Bodleian Library
UNIVERSITY OF OXFORD

This edition first published in 2013 by
the Bodleian Library
Broad Street
Oxford OX1 3BG

Reprinted in 2014

www.bodleianbookshop.co.uk

ISBN: 978 1 85124 086 9

This abridged edition © Bodleian Library, University of Oxford, 2013
First published in 1920 by Carmona & Baker, London, as *The Whole Art of
Dining with notes on the subject of service and table decorations*, by J. Rey.

Images adapted from illustrations in
*La Vie Parisienne*, 1918–1922, Oxford, Bodleian Library, Per. 2755 c.9;
*Picture Play*, 1928, Oxford, Bodleian Library, Per. 3858 d.2.

Cover design by Dot Little
Text designed and typeset in Gill Sans and ITC Bodoni Twelve
by illuminati, Grosmont
Printed and bound in China by C&C Offset Printing Co. Ltd
on 100 gsm YuLong pure 1.3 paper

British Library Catalogue in Publishing Data
A CIP record of this publication is available from the British Library

# CONTENTS

# PREFACE

At all the great social centres of the modern world, the art of dining wisely and yet well is one which must be thoroughly acquired by every host and hostess who aspires to distinction.

As the result of an ever-increasing refinement of luxury, the standard of good taste in entertaining has been greatly raised in recent years, becoming at the same time a matter of international convention, accepted alike in London, Paris, and New York.

To achieve a reputation in the giving of *recherché* dinner-parties now-a-days is to become in a sense an international celebrity. Small wonder, therefore, that the subject of dinners and dining is one of absorbing interest in Vanity Fair.

But to achieve distinction in these matters, something more is required than ample means and a well-ordered household.

The successful dinner, like every work of art, must present brainwork and imagination. No matter how efficient may be the head butler or Maître d'hôtel, the old adage of 'the master's eye' holds good. If entertaining is to be really well done, if it is to possess the enduring charms of spontaneity and infinite variety, it is essential that hosts and hostesses should take an intelligent personal interest in the arrangement of every detail. They must keep themselves thoroughly posted in the latest developments of the culinary art, and in the changing fashions of table decoration and equipment.

This work is written for reference and instruction in every particular connected with the all-important *Art of Dining* and the appointments of the *Modern Dinner-Table* for all occasions.

Such important matters as the correct laying of the covers, the choice of schemes of decoration, the proper serving of the various dishes, the skilful carving of joints and birds, the decanting and serving of fine wines, the preparation of menus, all these subjects are exhaustively dealt with and illustrated in this book.

Practical experience in the arrangement of high-class dinners and artistic table decorations for every kind of function, gained during many years' work at the most fashionable and best-appointed establishments, entitles me to speak with some authority on these subjects.

Private houses as well as public establishments differ so much in their circumstances and requirements, that it is impossible to draw up any generally applicable code of rules and regulations in connection with the table service and its arrangements; but the broad principles and general hints contained in this book are calculated to be of practical value, both to those who give orders and to those who carry them out, either in a private house or public establishment.

With this book in hand, even the most inexperienced person should be able to prepare a menu and to supervise the arrangements of the table for any function with very little difficulty, and with every prospect of satisfaction to all concerned.

*J. Rey*

# CHAPTER I

# THE DINING-ROOM

The dining-room, whether in a private house or in a public establishment, should always be at a temperature of 65° Fahrenheit an hour before a meal is to be served; this temperature should not be allowed either to rise or fall during meals; on the termination of each meal one or more windows should be thrown wide open so that perfect ventilation is effected before the next repast.

The luxury of the furniture and appointments of the dining-room of a private house depends, naturally, on the artistic taste of the owners and their social position; but more important than anything is scrupulous cleanliness of the room itself and of every article contained in it.

In the *restaurants de luxe* and the most up-to-date hotels, the colour of the dining-room carpet and curtains is generally red or pink, the walls and ceiling are painted with fine white enamel and embellished with gilt. This has for some time been the prevailing style in nearly all the first-class establishments throughout Europe.

The correct height of the tables in a restaurant or private dining-room is 28 inches, or 71 centimetres.

The space for each person's accommodation at a long banquet table or a large dinner-party depends on the number of guests and the available space of the table; in the case of space not being very great, a distance of at least 2 feet should be allowed between the centre of each plate; of course, whenever possible, it is better that this should be between 27 and 30 inches, as it affords more comfort to the guests.

In restaurants and dining-rooms of hotels, each waiter has (or should have) an *étagère*, or sideboard, fitted up with everything necessary for serving a meal properly, as this is essential for good service.

The most indispensable objects on the sideboard or serving-table are the following: an electric *réchaud*, or one with a spirit lamp for keeping the plates and dishes hot during the service, flat cold plates for cold meats, etc., small plates for cheese and sweets, salad plates, fruit plates, glass finger-bowls with their accompanying d'oyleys, a reserve number of large and small knives and forks, and silver fish and fruit knives, a sugar-basin containing soft sugar and another with lump sugar, each with its respective sifter and sugar-tongs, an oil and vinegar cruet, English and French mustard, and tooth-picks. If the restaurant or dining-room is a very spacious one, each waiter should provide himself with a certain number of bottles of the most frequently used sauces, such as Worcestershire, A.I, Harvey, Tomato Ketchup, Anchovy, etc.; for, if this is not done, a great deal of time is wasted by having to go for them during the serving of the meal.

In a small dining-room there is generally a small sideboard or table, either in the middle or corner of the room, containing all kinds of sauces, pickles, and condiments for the common use of all the waiters.

The dining-room carpet should be well swept once a day, preferably after the last meal at night, either with the *vacuum-cleaner*, or sprinkling it first with damp tea-leaves, so as to avoid raising any dust. Any crumbs left on the carpet after a meal should be taken up with a sweeping-machine, and care should be taken to open the windows wide at top and bottom, so that the room can be well ventilated and any smell of food got rid of.

# CHAPTER 2

# HOW TO LAY
# THE DINNER-TABLE

The first thing to be done before laying the table is to cover it with baize or a piece of thick soft cloth, so as to deaden the noise of the plates on the wood, to protect the arms from the edge of the table and to enable the cloth to hang better. With the tables of a restaurant this preliminary is not necessary, as a thick green baize is already nailed on each of the tables.

Before laying the table or tables, care must be taken that they stand straight and are perfectly even; and if by any chance one should have a leg shorter than another, the defect can be remedied by placing a small round cut from a bottle-cork under the short leg.

The method of laying the table, or rather, the manner of placing the plates, knives, forks, glasses, etc., is about the same everywhere. The difference between an ordinary family dinner-table and one arranged for a special occasion consists chiefly in the superior quality of the napery, china, silver, cut-glass, and flowers which adorn it, and on the artistic taste of the person who lays it.

The cloth should be put on with the greatest care so as not to show the least crease; the central fold running the length of the table exactly in the middle, each of the four corners being at exactly the same level; the size of the cloth being so that these corners do not drag on the floor nor yet hang too short.

The silver *epergne*, or the *corbeille* of flowers, should be placed exactly in the middle, with two candelabra with their corresponding candles and shades placed one on either side at equal distances from the centre and edges of the table (if set for from twelve to twenty places).

When the lights of the candelabra are not electric, the best to use are 'Arctic' lamps. These candelabra have the advantage of burning the candles right to the end whilst the shades remain at the same height as if the candles were always whole.

The flowers used for table decoration should be arranged with taste and with pleasing harmony of design calculated to charm the eyes of the guests.

All plates should be placed so that their edges are at the same distance—that is, half an inch from the edge of the table; the space between the centre of each plate should be from 24 to 30 inches.

In the houses of the aristocracy—especially in England—it was formerly the custom to lay each place with all the silver and knives necessary for each course, from the *Hors-d'œuvre* to the sweets. Besides this, there were heavy silver centres and candlesticks, fruit stands, and silver or gilt *cups*. This ostentation would be more becoming for the show-case of a silversmith than a dining-room table.

Fashion has changed all this for some time past, and nowadays at a well-arranged table it is customary to lay in each place nothing more than one large knife and fork, a silver fish-knife and fork, a soup spoon and an oyster-fork (if oysters are on the *menu*), or a small knife and fork for the *Hors-d'œuvre*.

At breakfast and luncheon, a small plate with a small steel knife for bread and butter is placed to the left of the central plate. Forks and spoons for sweets are no longer placed in front of the plates, this being considered very bad taste. Neither are large cruets or sauces or mustards placed on the table; these are handed round as required.

The number of glasses set for each person depends on the kinds of wine to be served.

The glasses generally used are the following: one for Sherry or Madeira, another for Hock or Rhine wine, a third for Bordeaux or Burgundy, and another for Champagne.

Liqueur glasses and Port-wine glasses should not be put on the table until these are to be served; nor glasses for water unless asked for during the meal for mixing Bordeaux or spirits with mineral water.

At a fashionable dinner, Port-wine and *vieux Bordeaux* are generally served with the sweets; therefore it is necessary to have glasses for these ready on the sideboard or on a silver tray, so that when the time comes they may be handed round without delay. Besides these, there should also be in reserve a number of glasses for water and liqueur as well as others for fine Champagne (called *verres à déguster*).

Whatever the number of wine glasses on a table may be (and this may be from one to eight according to the occasion and circumstances), they should be placed in front of each plate, a little to the right in the form of an opened fan or a triangle; the shorter ones (those for Sherry and Bordeaux) to the right, and the taller ones to the left of the group.

If special glasses are used for Hock or Rhine wine (tall coloured glasses), they should be placed at the most distant side of the group—in the middle or to the left preferably— so as to avoid the possibility of their being upset.

Only two glasses are put on restaurant tables that are not re served, namely one for Bordeaux and another for Champagne.

It is scarcely necessary to say here that knives and spoons should be laid to the right of the plate and forks to the left at about half an inch distant from the edge of the table. Neither is it necessary to advise that a good number of well-polished forks and knives should be kept in reserve from the beginning, in order to ensure adequate service at a dinner consisting of from ten to twelve courses.

Forks, spoons, or knives used for sweets, sherbets, fruit and ices are no longer put on the table beforehand crossed in front of the plates; this is an old custom and should be discontinued. These are now placed on their corresponding plates, or small silver tray, with a folded napkin to avoid noise, and are placed on the table when required.

It is superfluous to add here that at the breakfast or supper table spoons for soup, or fish knives and forks, are not laid unless these figure in the menu.

The custom of folding the table-napkins in fantastic shapes has gone out of use for some time past; the reason for this is that people object to use them when they have been so much handled.

Fantastically folded serviettes are now only seen in fifth-rate restaurants; but nevertheless it is still the custom at banquets to fold these in some simple shape, such as a mitre or a clown's cap, placed on the table or on the plates, but never in the glasses.

Between each two places a salt cellar and pepper-box or *moulin à poivre* should be placed, and in the centre of the table a *corbeille* of flowers artistically arranged with some kind of foliage such as smilax, asparagus fern, maidenhair fern, etc.

At a *recherché* dinner, neither butter nor *Hors-d'œuvre*, nor bottled sauces of any kind are placed on the table, but are handed on a silver tray when required.

Wine and mineral water bottles are always on the sideboard and should never be put on the table.

If there is much fruit, including perhaps pine-apples, peaches, muscatels, strawberries or *bigarroons*, and this is in a silver fruit stand, it may of course be placed on the table, but if so, care must be taken that it is in harmony with the candelabra, etc. When this is the case and the table at the same time is large and broad, the fruit-stands add greatly to the embellishment of the table.

Whatever plan of laying the table is adopted, care must be taken that the various articles of tableware are placed exactly to match each other on each side of the table parting from the centre.

# CHAPTER 3

# HINTS AND SUGGESTIONS IN
# FLORAL TABLE DECORATIONS

There are very few other occasions when so much combined artistic taste and skill are necessary as when decorating the table for a gala dinner-party. To do this really beautifully in various styles, all showing originality and exquisite taste, so as to command the attention of the guests, one should, of course, be an artist of consummate skill, as the attractiveness of the decorations and the value of the flowers depend upon the skilful manner in which they are arranged and displayed on the cloth.

Years ago, home floral decoration was practised by the ladies of the house, which must have been one of the most attractive and pleasant of household duties; and nowadays in small hotels where there is no special florist, this duty of decorating the tables still falls on the manager's wife, the housekeeper, or the head-waiter.

In the Hotels and Restaurants *de luxe* it is a general custom to decorate the tables with choice flowers daily; and this art has now reached such a point that very often the cost of the table decoration is greater than that of the meal itself.

Hostesses also are more than ever keen to get new ideas for their dinner-tables. A novel scheme of decoration, so long as it is not bizarre, gives a dinner-party a good start. It provides the guests with something to talk about at once, which is 'half the battle.' It strikes a note of distinction and taste which puts every one into a harmonious frame of mind.

The rivalry in the elegance and originality of the floral decorations is being pushed to such an extent by those who give the dinners that often fabulous sums are spent on rare flowers and skilled floral artists engaged to arrange them.

The old plan of trailing smilax on a table-centre or on the white cloth has given place to endless varieties of flower arrangements.

Care should be taken not to overload the table with flowers or silver or glass ornaments; for by so doing all impression of delicacy and elegance is lost. Skilled touch, a good eye for the combination of colours and exquisite taste are indispensable qualities in a florist in order to obtain an effect of admiration and appreciation among the guests.

Heavily scented flowers should not be used for table decoration.

In accordance with present-day fashion, the floral decoration of a ceremonious dinner should be with flowers of one colour and kind arranged with their own foliage. Nevertheless, white roses and red carnations or *vice-versa*, if they are well combined, give an exquisite effect.

One of the most popular foliages used for decorations is smilax, as it so easily lends itself to any kind of pretty effect on the cloth. Maidenhair fern and wild asparagus fern are also much in vogue, and with the majority of flowers give an exceedingly pretty effect.

Small silver or bronze ornaments or *statuettes* representing rustic figures or cupids placed here and there among the flowers add greatly to the beauty of the decoration and form a pleasing contrast.

At dinners of etiquette it is customary to place before each cover the name of the guest written on a small card representing either a rose-leaf, a little boat, an oyster-shell, a fish, a vine-leaf, a round of lemon, etc., and these also add greatly to the embellishment of the table.

In large establishments—and in many small ones also—where the *pâtissiers* are real artists, the *corbeilles en sucre*, in which the *petits-fours* are served, are splendid substitutes for real flowers when these are scarce in winter.

Before laying the table and getting the flowers, the kind and colour of these must be ascertained; for the candle-shades, as well as the furniture of the room where the dinner is given, must be in harmony with them, or no good effect can be obtained.

Silk and embroidered table-centres and massive silver *epergnes*, formerly always used in private houses, are now quite out of fashion. To-day a light silver flower-stand, or a bowl of brilliantly tinted sweet peas or hot-house roses, is considered to be the most elegant and appropriate centre-piece. The stand should be of a delicate rustic design, with several branches; the central and larger one not being so high as to impede the view of the guests; also an artistic high lamp gives a nice effect.

If the table is laid for more than twelve places, two smaller stands of the same type should be placed on either side of the centre one; but if two candelabra are on the table, these small stands must be placed outside these at equal distances from the ends of the table.

On a really elegantly arranged table for a fashionable dinner nothing should be placed beyond the covers for each person; that is, the plates, silver, glasses, bread and serviettes; the salt-cellars, pepper-boxes, candlesticks, and the flowers in the centre.

*Hors-d'œuvre*, fruit, water, butter, mustard, cruets, etc., should never be put on an elegantly arranged table; otherwise *l'éclat* or the splendour of its style is lost.

It has already been remarked that the serviettes or table-napkins are no longer folded in fantastic shapes; this custom has long died out in first-class establishments. If the serviettes are embroidered in relief with the family monogram, the best way is to leave them folded on the plates with the monogram on the upper side and a roll in the folds in the middle.

However, in an establishment where economy has to be observed, and perhaps no new and elegant set of silver or the necessary flowers are available, one has to make the best of what the material and circumstances afford. In this case a very pretty effect may be obtained with the fruit placed carefully in the silver stands, and embellished with vine leaves, or in fancy baskets with moss.

The design of the decoration depends naturally on the kind and quantity of flowers, and on the kind of ornaments and flower stands available. If these latter are modern and of beautiful design, few flowers should be used, but great care must be taken that these are arranged with their foliage in the most artistic and delicate manner possible.

Another pretty way (especially with fine tinted roses) is to wire them and stick them into a flat receptacle filled with wet sand covered with moss, placed in the centre of the table. This gives them an absolutely natural appearance, as if they had grown on the cloth.

If there is a lamp hanging from the ceiling over the centre of the table, this may be made use of to suspend from it four trails of smilax with china roses or primroses interlaced. The ends of the trails may be fastened either to the corners of the table with drawing-pins or secured with the candlesticks or any other ornament.

When a dinner is given in honour of the birthday of one of the young ladies of the house, it is a pretty idea, if violets or any small flowers are very plentiful, to form with these some suitable words of greeting on the cloth, such as 'Good Wishes', etc., or if the table is a long one, the familiar old birthday wish, 'Many happy returns of the day.' On such an occasion, this cannot do otherwise than please. The words, of course, may be made to refer to any other person at a similar gathering.

Very small fairy electric lights of various colours, in harmony with the foliage and flowers, also make a charming decoration and give a very brilliant effect.

These little lamps are about the size of an olive and are linked together on a fine electric wire with a small space between them. They can be formed up into almost any design on the cloth, care being taken to interlace them with the smilax.

The lights used for the dinner-table form an important subject. A safe and pleasant light is absolutely necessary for the comfort of the guests' eyes.

The old-fashioned wax candles of guttering propensity which so often alarmed the guests and were most annoying to the hostess during dinner, by the ornamental shades taking fire, have long disappeared from all well-appointed tables.

Electric lamps are clean and artistic for table illumination, but have a drawback: they cannot be used unless the establishment is fitted with electric light; also the electric cord often stands in the way of the diners or servants and causes accidents.

The most suitable and by far the best table light is obtainable with the 'Arctic' lamps. These are a novel form of candle-holders in outward appearance resembling fine wax candles. They are constructed on the same principle as a carriage or reading-lamp, in which the candle, enclosed in a metal tube, is forced up as it burns by means of a spiral spring inside.

They are clean, safe, and simple to refill, and allow the candles to be burnt to the very end; yet in appearance they do not vary in height.

They are most artistic looking, give a soft and even light, and lend themselves to the most delightful arrangement of greenery and flower decoration.

At a fashionable dinner it is customary to place a *buttonhole* in the place of each gentleman, and a *spray* in each lady's place. These are put in front of or to the right of each cover. They are provided with pins; for the ladies a black-headed one about 3 inches long to pin the spray easily to the dress, and with the buttonholes a shorter pin about 1½ inches for the gentlemen to pin them to the left buttonhole of their coat.

Flowers at a Wedding breakfast are invariably white, and the *statuettes* must be appropriate to the occasion; as little cupids armed with bow and arrows, silver horseshoes, or horseshoes formed with white flowers (these are popularly supposed to bring

good luck), and the whole table may be lightly sprinkled with golden confetti and little gold and silver horseshoes.

These pretty little horseshoes are made of cardboard covered with silver and gilt paper, and can be obtained in boxes at any shop where articles for the table are sold.

The wedding-cake, usually very large, is placed in the centre of the table in front of the bride and bridegroom.

The bride's bouquet is placed on the table before her during the luncheon.

The most frequently used flowers for table decoration (other than weddings) are Roses and Carnations of all kinds and colours, Parma violets, Lilies of the valley, Lavender in branches, Mimosa, Mignonette, different kinds of Orchids, Heliotrope, Lilac, Jonquils, China and Wichuriana wild roses, Sweet Peas, Daffodils, Wallflowers, Tulips, Ghent Azaleas, Primroses, Peach and Almond blossoms, etc.

Wild flowers, such as Daisies, Poppies and Forget-me-nots, can also be advantageously employed, especially in country houses or on some campestral occasion, and they all lend themselves naturally to an infinity of designs on the cloth.

The white tablecloth, by the way, has been out of favour for some time amongst those who lead the fashion upon artistic lines. A beautiful table is too good to be hidden. Silver and glass show up exquisitely against oak or Spanish mahogany or polished walnut. In many of the houses possessing a costly and beautiful dinner-table the tablecloth is replaced by pretty d'oyleys and round mats of rich lace, placed before each guest, and a design is built up most elaborately. These tables usually have a thick sheet of glass on top to prevent spoiling the polish with the hot plates and dishes.

A novel and most effective decoration may also be made with water-plants and water-lilies, placed in a special tin painted either white or green, of oval shape, about 2 inches deep to hold the water. The size of the tin must be in proportion to that of the table; and the plants, flowers and green leaves, etc., must be made to represent an aquatic garden.

For this decoration scheme an automatic fountain playing, made of cut-glass mounted in silver as in the illustration, is essential.

These fountains are about 2 feet in height and are placed in the centre of the table.

By a mechanical spring, the colour of the water spray is continually changing, and the effect is marvellously beautiful.

The makers of these table fountains are Messrs. Laing & Wharton, Ltd., London.

# CHAPTER 4

# GENERAL RULES TO BE OBSERVED BEFORE AND WHILE WAITING AT TABLE

The first duty of the waiter in a restaurant, or the butler in a private house, is to see that everything on the table is scrupulously clean and polished; that is to say, the tablecloth, plates, glasses, knives, forks, etc. Also to see that the salt-cellars and pepper-boxes are properly filled, the mustard freshly made, and that every requisite for the service of a meal, whether breakfast, lunch, dinner, or supper is quite ready beforehand, so as not to cause pauses and delays during the service.

The plates should be either very hot or very cold according to their use.

All food should be served at the left-hand side of the guests (except in the case of a person being so near the wall or a pillar that it is impossible to serve on that side).

Coffee, sugar and bread are also served at the left; but wines, liqueurs, water and ice in glasses are served at the right hand.

Glasses and cups should never be filled to the brim.

Before serving Champagne, all empty Sherry, Rhine wine or Chablis glasses should be removed from the table and placed on a medium-sized silver tray carried in the left hand.

On clearing away the glasses care must be taken not to put the fingers in them. This is tolerated only in a tavern.

As soon as Champagne is served the Bordeaux glasses must be removed unless any of the guests prefer Bordeaux to Champagne.

The dishes, before being carried to the table, should be wiped with a cloth, in case the bottoms or edges should not be quite clean. On handing the dishes, the waiter or servant should turn his face from the person he is waiting upon and try to retain his breath as much as possible.

At a grand dinner, the dirty plates of one course should not be removed until all (or nearly all) the guests have finished.

A waiter in a hotel or restaurant, when speaking to his customers or receiving orders from them, should stand in a correct attitude and not lean on one side, nor put his hands in his pockets, nor on the table, nor on the back of the chair, nor anything of the kind.

Before beginning to wait at lunch or dinner in a hotel or restaurant, a waiter should study well the *carte du jour* and the *menu*, so as to be perfectly acquainted with the technicalities of the dishes and of their composition, in order to be able to reply immediately and correctly to any questions on the subject put to him by his customers.

A waiter who cannot answer the questions that may be asked him as to the composition of the dishes on the *carte du jour* or *menu* is looked upon as being stupid and ignorant of his profession; for, even though the customer may not verbally express this opinion, yet he thinks it all the same.

In a hotel or restaurant, the Maître d'hôtel sees to the allocation of the tables and assigns places to the customers; and in the case of an important or special personage, the Maître d'hôtel receives his orders and passes them on to the waiter. Residents in a hotel, dining at the *table d'hôte*, give their orders straight to the waiter. In a restaurant where there is only one Maître d'hôtel, the waiters themselves receive the orders unless the Maître d'hôtel wishes to show special attention to some distinguished *habitué*.

If a client finds fault with a dish or anything else, the waiter should never argue with him, but inform the Maître d'hôtel directly, who will see that it is rectified, and smooth matters over with the customer (if he is angry); thereby probably evading complaints to the manager. It is the Maître d'hôtel who is responsible for everything concerning the service in the restaurant; therefore it is to him that the waiter should go when in trouble with a difficult customer; for the Maître d'hôtel, with tact gained by long experience in the profession, understands better how to appease and satisfy certain impatient or bad-tempered clients, and avoids complaints which to the ordinary waiter would be almost impossible.

While waiting at table the waiter should be continually on the alert, serving each dish and its accompanying requisites at the proper time, such as gravy, sauce, vegetables or salad, without allowing his customers to wait or ask for anything.

Waiters should train their eye to see that bread, butter, ice, water, etc., are within reach of the customers; also serve the sauces or mustards when required without being asked.

If a certain dish on the *carte* is finished half-way through lunch or dinner, the Kitchen-clerk should make this known by writing up the name of the dish or dishes at the entrance of the kitchen, so that the waiters may see it; and these should immediately cross it off the *carte* or menu to avoid dissatisfaction with the customers.

On receiving an order for a steak or mutton chop, the customer should be asked if *well done* or *under-done* is desired, and this must be noted on the kitchen *check* for the guidance of the *rôtisseur*. In this way many altercations between the employees and complaints from customers are avoided.

If a chop or steak is not cooked according to the customer's wish and he tells the waiter of it, he should remove the plate without remarks, rectify the fault if possible, or courteously and respectfully offer something else in its place. The same thing should be done with respect to any other dish; and if the fault lies with the kitchen, the chef should be told, but without any particular opinion being passed or any offensive remarks made, for it is absolutely indispensable that perfect harmony should exist between the kitchen employees and those in the dining-room.

A similar precaution also applies to boiled eggs, and it is superfluous to give the reason why.

Directly an order is taken and noted on the check (whether *à la carte* or *table d'hôte*) this must be sent to the kitchen and the *Hors-d'œuvre* served at once.

In a large restaurant there are several *sommeliers* or butlers, especially to serve the wines, and these should present the list to the customers directly the kitchen order has been given, or the wine-list may be left on the table at the host's left side, if he is not disposed to order immediately. If there are no special wine-butlers, then the ordinary waiter takes the order himself.

Great care should be exercised when taking orders for wines. First of all the waiter should make sure that the order-number on the left side of the wine-list corresponds with the wine ordered by the customer, and should note it on the wine check; secondly, he should make sure whether a whole or only half bottle is required; because once a bottle is uncorked, the waiter is obliged to make good any error from his own pocket, as well as to hear uncomplimentary remarks from the management.

If *red* wine is ordered, the customer should be asked if he desires it at the temperature of the cellar or warmed; and in the case of *white* wine, if cooled or otherwise; for although these should be served at quite different temperatures, the customers' taste varies infinitely in a public restaurant.

When mineral waters are served, the bottles should be opened outside the dining-room to prevent accidents; for it often happens that a lady's dress or gentleman's shirt-front is spoiled through the clumsy manipulation of these by the waiter.

It is better to place mineral water bottles and syphons ready for mixing wines, whisky or cognac on the table at the right hand of a customer, so that he may help himself to his taste; otherwise there is a risk of pouring either too much or not enough.

At a *table d'hôte* lunch or dinner in a hotel, the dishes are handed once only, unless one is asked for again by a diner; but at a restaurant, *à la carte*, they are offered a second time (if anything is left in them).

Customers dining alone are best served by putting the dishes on the table in front of them.

When serving a party of two *à la carte*, the waiter should put the dish and plates on one side of the table, cut and serve nice neat portions himself, and place the plates in front of the party; serving the lady first and then the gentleman.

It has already been mentioned that a good waiter must be intelligent, alert, and thoroughly conversant with all the different kinds of sauces and requisites accompanying a particular dish, such as *chutney* with *curry*, *mint sauce* with roast lamb, *red currant jelly* with venison or roast mutton, etc., so as to be able to serve them quickly without being asked for same.

A large spoon and fork must accompany the vegetable dishes for the customers to help themselves. For some vegetables, such as boiled potatoes, peas, spinach, etc., only a spoon is necessary.

All dishes must be held close to the customer's plate to avoid anything being spilt on the table-cloth, and scrupulous cleanliness must be observed with everything.

When not actually waiting, the waiter should stand in readiness two or three yards distant from the table; and if his customers are engaged in conversation, he must be quite indifferent to it.

Plates must be changed from the left-hand side, and fresh knives and forks must be carried to the table on a large plate or tray with a folded serviette beneath them to avoid noise.

To do everything as silently as possible must be the aim of every efficient waiter—not only in his movements at the table in changing the plates, handing the dishes, etc., but in all his movements in the room. If there is no carpet in the dining-room or restaurant, he must take great care not to make a noise in walking on the parquet. This can best be avoided by wearing either rubber heels to his ordinary shoes or by procuring a pair of special flexible shoes for waiters.

Strict watch must be kept on the table to see if any customer is in need of anything, such as bread, butter, toast, ice, etc., to pass it immediately and to fill the wine-glasses with the wine proper to each course.

Bread must on no account be touched with the hands; it should be passed to the diners on a small silver basket or on a plate with a folded serviette on it. Household bread should be cut in even squares.

Letters or any small article should also be handed to a customer on a small silver tray.

It is quite unnecessary to add in conclusion that strict personal cleanliness and perfect neatness in clothes and shoes must always be observed.

One other observation might here be made. The cloth or serviette carried by the waiter is to be used first to polish the table ware, to protect the hands from the hot dishes, and to polish the dinner-plates; it must *not* be used for dusting the furniture (as is often the case) or any other purpose whatsoever.

# CHAPTER 5

# ORDER IN WHICH THE GUESTS SHOULD BE SERVED AT TABLE

At the family table in a private house the mother or lady of the house is served first, then the young ladies in succession, according to age, and the governess last (if present); then the father and sons, beginning with the eldest.

At a small dinner-party, if the table is laid for not more than six covers, *i.e.*, three ladies and three gentlemen, one dish will suffice, and this is handed first to the lady on the host's right hand, then to the lady on his left. The hostess (who generally sits facing the host) is always served last of all the ladies. The gentlemen follow beginning with those on the right and left hand of the hostess. The host is served last unless any of his sons are present.

At a large dinner consisting of many covers, where each course is served in several dishes, the two ladies on either side of the host are served simultaneously, and the rest of the guests are served in the order as they are seated, regardless of sex.

In order to ensure good and efficient service one waiter or servant should not attend to more than six guests, and he must take care to begin to hand each course with the guest last served with the preceding one. For example, if the dinner consists of 50 or 100 or more covers, each waiter should begin to serve the *Hors-d'œuvre* to his party proceeding from left to right, and then begin with the soup where he left off with the *Hors-d'œuvre*, and so on to the end of the meal. The two waiters who are serving the two ladies on the right and left of the host always begin with these and then keep the same order as the other waiters, always, of course, serving the host last.

It used to be the custom at large dinner-parties always to serve the ladies before the gentlemen; but the method just explained is the one usually followed now in large houses and first-class hotels and restaurants. It has the great advantage over the old style in that there is no risk of confusion and delay as was often the case with the former.

At a large banquet, one waiter has to attend to six, eight, or ten guests according to the importance of the banquet; but the one waiting on the chairman usually attends only to three and never more than five covers. He always begins with the chairman, follows with the two guests on the chairman's right hand and then the two on his left alternately. The rest of the waiters start serving from left to right of their party, taking care to begin to serve each course where the previous one finished.

Although it is the general rule for the guests to help themselves, a dexterous waiter can do so, if it is preferred, by holding the dish with his left hand and serve with the right. This involves a little ability in manipulating both the spoon and fork together with only one hand; but this is nothing to a trained waiter.

# CHAPTER 6

# THE DENOMINATIONS
# OF THE FRENCH DISHES
# AND THEIR ORIGIN

Although the majority of gourmets and caterers have a good knowledge of culinary matters, it cannot be said the same of them with regard to the denominations of the French dishes and their origin; consequently I think the present occasion a good one to give a little *aperçu* on this interesting subject.

First of all, it must be observed that the main object of the different denominations figuring on the menus is to show the distinction that exists between the various ways of preparing the dishes.

By this means, the Maître d'hôtel, or the waiter, on receiving his customer's order, noting it on the kitchen check, can convey to the chef the exact way in which the dishes must be prepared. On the other hand they serve to convey to the host and his guests a knowledge of how the different dishes are cooked and will be served in the course of the repast.

Nearly all the names of dishes have an authentic origin, not at all difficult to trace, and they are not, as is often believed, the offspring of the cook's fancy for the moment; although occasionally a cook, through some unforeseen circumstance, or in some cases because he wants to differ from other people, will send up a dish with a name that does not really belong to it. This should never be done; because not only is it an infringement of the rules governing the culinary art which a good chef will always respect, but it leads to endless confusion throughout the service, preventing all harmony and understanding between those who receive and write the orders in the dining-room or restaurant, and those who execute them in the kitchen.

There must be perfect accord between the Maître d'hôtel and the chef, and these together should most rigorously observe and see that those under them observe the established rules of the culinary art in this respect.

No fantastic name should be given to a dish either on the order check or on the menu, and every dish should be prepared and garnished exactly in accordance with its denomination.

These denominations are many and various. Some get their origin from an historical event: an edict, a treaty, a celebrated battle or a famous victory; such as *à la Nantes*, *à la Sainte Alliance*, *à la Marengo*, *à la Turbigo*, etc. (See chapter on 'History and Biographical Notices of Distinguished Epicures' in *Le Guide du Gourmet à Table*.)

Dishes called after famous epicures or poet-*gourmets*, as *Brillat-Savarin, Alexandre Dumas, Berchoux, Richelieu, Lucullus*, etc., are prepared in accordance with the rule established by those personages.

If a dish figures on the menu as being *à l'Anglaise*, *à l'Espagnole*, *à la Russe*, or *à la Française*, etc., it is understood that the dish is prepared according to the method of cooking in the country from which it takes its name.

Occasionally a dish is named after a King, a Queen, or a member of the Royal Family; such as *Victoria*, *Alexandra*, *Edward VII*, *Alfonso XIII*, *Dauphine*, *Prince de Galles*, *d'Orléans*, etc.; others are simply called *à la Reine*, *à la Royale*, *à la Tzarina*, or *à l'Impérial*.

Again, dishes are frequently named after contemporary celebrities, as at the present day the names of Mesdames *Patti*, *Melba*, *Réjane* and *Sarah Bernhardt* often figure on the menu.

Numerous dishes also bear the names of famous *chefs* who invented them; such as *Carème*, *Voisin*, *Dugléré*, *Marguery*, etc.

The dishes named after *Mesdames Montespan*, *de Maintenon* and *Louis XIV*, and those called *à la Du Barry*, *Pompadour*, and *Louis XV*, are, according to history, the inventions of the favourites of those two kings; who, being well versed in culinary matters, invented and otherwise turned their attention to composing delicate dishes with which to whet the jaded appetites of their royal lovers.

# CHAPTER 7

# THE ART OF
# COMPOSING A MENU

To the eminent Brillat-Savarin is attributed the saying, 'To know how to eat and drink with discernment is a science which belongs only to epicures gifted with a refined taste.' And as a corollary it may be added that to know how to draw up a menu properly, so as to tempt epicures to indulge pleasurably in dainty dishes, is an art which belongs only to those gifted with gastronomic discernment, backed up by a practical knowledge of the culinary art.

I propose to throw a little much-needed light on the subject of menu composition. First of all, then, the success of a dinner of importance is not entirely due to the correct and skilful way in which the dishes are cooked and presented, but in no small measure to their harmonious arrangement on the menu.

*Menu mal fait, diner perdu,* so runs an old French proverb; indicating that if the dishes are not judiciously chosen and their order not wisely arranged, the repast cannot be satisfactory from an epicurean standpoint.

To draw up a menu for an important dinner is not an easy matter, as some inexperienced people are inclined to believe; it is an art that is only acquired by long experience gained in the best schools. I have often seen menus composed by people quite competent in other branches of the Hotel and Restaurant business that showed a lamentable ignorance of the rules which govern menu composition.

The dinner menu of to-day is not the result of custom or fashion altogether, but has gradually been evolved from the scientific study of the true needs of the digestion.

The *Hors-d'œuvre* is meant to stimulate the flow of saliva in the mouth, it being of a salty nature, and to warn the various digestive organs to get ready.

According to Carème and other savants in culinary matters, soup, that is, a solution of meat extract in hot water, is the greatest digestive stimulant known to physiologists.

Fish and Entrées, both soft-fibred and of easily digestible articles, lead up to the heavy meats and vegetables, which are the relatively indigestible filling part of a meal.

Game serves to tickle the waning appetite and satisfy the last remains of hunger.

Savoury is the final salty stimulus to the flagging digestion.

The menu of a dainty dinner, or that of a sumptuous banquet, should only be drawn up after careful meditation as to its composition and due consideration of the numerous details which have to be taken into account. The menu, of course, is more or less long and more or less varied, according to the price to be spent on the dinner and the number of diners. At a dinner-party where the guests are mostly ladies, and money is not a prime consideration, the fare should be of a delicate character, and the number of dishes never in excess of eight—*viz. Hors-d'œuvre*, Oysters or Melon—Clear or thick soup—Fillets of sole or trout cooked in a dainty and attractive manner—Lamb noisettes or *Medaillons de Bœuf aux primeurs*—then, either Chicken, Poussin, Pheasant, Quails or Ortolans *en Cocotte*, and a green salad—Asparagus or some other nice vegetable—and a hot or cold sweet, such as pudding soufflé or cabinet, *Omelette en surprise*, *macédoine de fruits glacée aux liqueurs*, Trifle, Peaches, Pears or Strawberries Melba, and Friandises.

Plain fruit, such as Grapes, Pineapple, Peaches, etc., is always placed in the centre of the table and does not, of course, count as a dish.

At a dinner or banquet where the guests are mainly gentlemen, the menu should provide a greater number of dishes of more satisfying nature and marked flavour, and in the following order:

HORS-D'ŒUVRE may consist of an assortment of Sardines, Anchovies, Olives, Radishes, various salads, smoked Salmon, Westphalian Ham, etc., or Caviare, Oysters, Cantaloup Melon, and pheasant or plovers' eggs when in season.

POTAGE: Two soups are generally provided on the menu, one clear (usually turtle soup or *Petite marmite*) and a *velouté* or cream soup; but one of these only is served to each individual diner.

POISSON: At a big dinner it is customary to serve two kinds of fish; the first is always a large plain boiled fish, such as salmon, turbot, cod, or brill, accompanied by new boiled potatoes and Hollandaise or Mousseline sauce. The second fish is either whitebait, fried smelts, or fillets of sole *en goujons*.

ENTRÉE: As everybody knows, this consists either of fowl, sweetbread, *Foie gras*, *mousse de jambon* or *de canard*, or any kind of game that may be in season, cooked in an elaborate manner and served with a rich sauce.

RELEVÉ: This, in culinary parlance, is the name given in France to the course following the fish, which, being the butcher's meat, is also known as *la pièce de résistance*. In plain English this is the remove, or—

JOINT: It can be safely said that there is scarcely a banquet or a large dinner which does not embrace either a joint of beef, a braised ham, or a saddle of mutton, lamb, or venison. Potatoes and two green vegetables, at least, are served with them. It may here be mentioned, by the way, that the joint or butcher's meat has rather a changeable place on the menu. In France, as said before, it is generally served immediately after the fish (following Brillat-Savarin's ideas, 'first solid food, then the more delicate one'), and is called the *relevé*. In England, however, the joint is served between the *entrée* and the *Sorbet*. This is, of course, a matter of taste or individual preference.

The joint is followed by a kind of *entr'acte*, in which is served:

PUNCH À LA ROMAINE: This may be replaced, if desired, either by a *sorbet au citron*, *neige au Clicquot*, or *granité au champagne*. At this course, gentlemen generally smoke a Russian cigarette.

RÔTI: For this course tame or wild birds are usually required. They comprise turkeys, capons, ducks, chicken, poussins, pheasants, partridges, grouse, quails, larks and ortolans, accompanied by their corresponding gravy and a nicely dressed salad.

SALADE: This should be a plain one. The next course is the—

LÉGUME: Whatever is in season. Asparagus, either English or French, are always well received at any table; besides there are other very nice vegetables, such as *Fonds d'Artichauts à l'Italienne, Petits pois à la Française, Haricots verts nouveaux au Beurre, Aubergines à l'Egyptienne, Cardons et célery à la Moëlle*, Sea-kale, new Carrots, Salsifis, and *Fèves à la crème.* Following the vegetable comes the—

ENTREMET: This consists, as a rule, of a hot pudding of some sort, or an *Omelette Soufflée* or *en Surprise, Croûtes aux Ananas, Crème renversée*, etc., and is followed by the—

GLACE: There is a large variety of ices, both water ice and cream ice; they are known by such denominations as *Asperges glacées, Biscuits* and *Châteaubriands glacés, Pêches à la vanille, Coupes Jacques, Gauffrettes, Mandarines en surprise*, and *Bombes*. With the ice it is customary to serve wafers, *Petits Fours*, or Friandises. The ice is followed by the—

SAVOURY: Such as anchovies, caviare, sardines, soft roes, and mushrooms served on small buttered toasts; also haddock and cheese soufflées, Scotch woodcock, Welsh-rarebits, etc.

Last of all comes the dessert; then coffee and liqueurs.

When choosing the edibles for a dinner it is of the utmost importance to see that they are in season and therefore at their best. If tinned or other provisions not in season are introduced, these are sure to compromise the success of the repast; and since every edible is seasonable for a certain length of time during the year, these should be chosen when in their prime (see Chapter 23).

The selection of the dishes must be made very carefully; it is necessary to bear in mind their appearance, and the contrast that should exist amongst them. Also that each is not only of a different nature, but involves various methods of cooking.

The same vegetables or garnishes must not appear twice on the same menu, except only truffles and mushrooms; these two are always welcome.

The sauces employed for garnishing and for masking the cooked dishes, as well as those served separately, must not only be different in character, but also varied in colour.

On drafting a French menu (French is universally recognised to be the language for both menus and *cuisine*), care should be exercised not to introduce in it English expressions, as is often done, or if written in English, to avoid unnecessary French terms, as with a little thought it is quite possible to give in English the French equivalents; otherwise a menu is as absurd as it is incongruous.

The French locution *à la* is also often misused when writing menus in French. It should be used only when it is meant that a particular dish is cooked after the fashion or style of a country; such as: *à la Française—à la Russe—à la Marengo*, etc.

When a dish has been dedicated to a personage, the locution *à la* should be left out altogether; as *Consommé Sarah-Bernhardt*, *Sole Colbert*, and *Pêches Melba*.

I do not consider it necessary to draw up a specimen menu here, as I have done so at the end of every meal, in its corresponding chapter. With the instructions given above and the numerous dishes at the end of this book, any person, inexperienced as he or she may be, will be able to solve the problem of correct menu compilation.

To sum up, the art of composing or drawing up a menu consists, first, in choosing with discrimination the edibles and the dishes that go to make up the dinner; secondly, in distributing and combining them harmoniously with due regard to their gastronomic value and digestibility.

# CHAPTER 8

# BREAKFAST

As is generally known, breakfast on the Continent is a very light meal, consisting only of a cup of chocolate or coffee and milk with some toast and butter or a roll, and just occasionally with boiled eggs.

In England and in the United States, the breakfast is an extensive meal and somewhat complicated to serve.

The method of laying the table for breakfast in England is the following:

To each cover lay a large steel knife and silver fish-knife to the right with their corresponding forks to the left, and a medium-sized spoon for porridge to the right of the knives, a fruit plate with d'oyley and finger-bowl, and fruit knife and fork (the English and American custom being to begin breakfast with fresh fruit),

# BREAKFAST MENU

## ENGLISH STYLE

Tea, Coffee, Cocoa,
Chocolate, Malted Milk

———

Fresh Fruit assorted
Stewed Fruit

———

Porridge and Cream

———

### FISH
Grilled Mackerel
Grilled Turbot
Fried Soles
Finnon Haddock
Kippers
Bloaters
Grilled Fresh Herrings
Kedgeree
Fish cakes

———

Fried Eggs and Bacon
Plain Omelette
Ham and Eggs
Poached Eggs on Toast
Grilled Kidneys
Calf's Liver and Bacon
Grilled Gammon Rasher
Sausages and
Mashed Potatoes
Grilled Tomatoes and Bacon
Grilled Mushrooms on Toast

———

### TO ORDER
*Ready in 20 minutes*
Mutton Chops
Chump Chops
Rump Steak
Lamb or Mutton Cutlets
Kidneys Vert-Pré

———

### COLD BUFFET
Roast Beef
Lamb
Mutton
Galantine
York Ham
Ox Tongue
Chicken
Pressed-Beef

———

Muffins, Crumpets
Honey, Jam, Marmalade

# BREAKFAST MENU

## AMERICAN STYLE

Iced Melon, Grape-fruit
Apples, Pears, Grapes
Radishes, Olives, Water-cress
Creamed Oats, Boiled Sago
Hominy, Force
Cracked Wheat
Shredded Wheat Biscuits
Corn-on-Cob
Grape Nuts and Cream
Buckwheat and Golden Syrup

---

### FISH

Panned Blue Points
Broiled Whitefish
Grilled Salmon Steak
Planked Shad
Fish Rolls

---

Buttered Eggs
Poached Eggs
Parsley Omelette

---

Baked Beans
Scotch Pie
Irish-stew
Beef-Hash
Curried Mutton

---

### TO ORDER

*Ready in 20 minutes*
Sirloin Steak and
Fried Potatoes
Sheep's Liver and Bacon
Grilled Ham
Mutton Cutlets
Pork Chops

---

Corned-Beef
Ox-Tongue
Veal and Ham Pie

---

Hominy Cakes
Hominy Fritters
Oaten Biscuits
Preserves
Buttered Toast
Hot Rolls and Crackers

39

a small plate with the serviette and a roll with a small steel knife for butter to the left of the cover. To the right place a large cup and saucer (*called breakfast-cup*).

In the centre of the table place two sugar basins, one containing lump sugar and the other castor sugar, a cruet, iced water, and various kinds of fresh fruit according to season.

The first thing to be served to American visitors staying in a hotel is iced water, followed by melon or grape-fruit (prepared beforehand).

The Grape-fruit is a kind of pale yellow orange, of slightly acid taste, much resembling a large Californian lemon. The method of preparing and serving these is the following: First, cut the fruit in halves and with a small sharp knife cut out the centre where the pips are, in the shape of a cone, and place them on a dish. When each fruit is thus prepared on the dish, place this in a refrigerator or on crushed ice, as they should be served as cold as possible.

In a hotel where a complete staff is employed this operation would be performed by whoever has charge of the fruit.

With the Grape-fruit castor sugar is served. These are also served at dinner as *Hors-d'œuvre*, with castor sugar and Port-wine poured in them.

After the fruit comes the Porridge, which is also served with castor sugar and cream or milk.

Next comes one of the various kinds of fish figuring on the menu, and these are usually fried sole, bloaters, kippers, grilled herrings, etc.

Following the fish is the characteristic English dish of fried eggs and bacon. Then, according to the appetite of the diner, is served a chop or beefsteak with potatoes, or cold meat.

As a general rule, breakfast is finished with honey or some preserve as marmalade, etc., or *compôte* of fruit (if this is not served at the beginning of the meal, as is frequently the case). In English hotels there is always a large variety of *compôte* of fruit (fresh and preserved) kept in readiness on the buffet during breakfast.

As regards bread, instead of placing a roll on each cover, it is sometimes more convenient to place a silver basket or in place of this an ordinary plate with a serviette on the centre of the table containing an assortment of rolls, crescents and *brioches*, so that the customer may choose what he pleases. Butter and toast should always be on the table without waiting for a customer to ask for them.

In the hotels of North America it is the custom to serve an endless variety of cereals at breakfast.

The Breakfast Menus shown on the preceding pages are typical of England and North America.

# CHAPTER 9

# LUNCHEON

Luncheon in private houses on the Continent is served between twelve and one o'clock.

In the hotels and restaurants of Europe in general *Le Déjeuner à la Fourchette* is served between half-past twelve and two p.m.

The menu of the *Déjeuner à la Fourchette* is generally composed of *Hors-d'œuvre variés* or soup, followed by either fish or eggs, a lightly prepared meat dish such as *Navarin aux Primeurs*, Goulash, calf's head, tongue and spinach, etc.; grilled meat such as *Entrecôte*, mutton chops, etc., and salad, sweets, cheese, fruit, etc.

In all the first-class restaurants there is always a *Buffet Froid* during luncheon containing a large selection of cold meats for the choice of the customers.

Anything taken from the buffet is generally served in place of a dish figuring on the menu, consequently there is no extra charge for this, unless it is some very special thing and correspondingly expensive.

The following is the method of laying the table for luncheon: To each cover, a small plate with folded serviette and a roll placed upon it; a large steel knife and a silver fish knife on the right and their corresponding forks on the left; a small steel knife for butter placed on a small plate on the left, and a large soup spoon (if there is soup) on the right; a small knife and fork crossed on the centre plate if *Hors-d'œuvre* figure on the menu.

The old custom of laying a small knife, fork and spoon crossed before the plate, is no longer observed in modern establishments.

Butter should not be placed on the table until beginning to serve the meal, and care must be taken that this is quite hard. In the summer it is advisable to place a small piece of ice in each butter-dish.

Before being sent to table it is formed into fancy shapes such as twists, small round balls, medallions or pats stamped with either a flower, a dairy-maid, or the name of the establishment. When thus prepared it is placed in a large earthen bowl filled with iced water ready to be served when wanted. In each small butter-dish should be placed not more than two small balls or one medallion for each person, and the dishes placed on a small plate with a d'oyley and a special butter knife on one side.

In summer the custom is to frequently serve 'Cold Luncheon', consisting of cold roast beef and pickles, or fowl and ham with salad, cheese, bread and butter.

Luncheon, like dinner, is served *à la Russe*, this being the universal practice in all up-to-date establishments.

In an establishment where no 'wine-butlers' are kept the waiter has to take the orders for wine and serve it himself.

When opening the bottles care must be taken to remove every vestige of wire or capsule that might adhere to the neck, and wipe the mouth of the bottle well. Before taking the wine to the table it is as well to pour out just a little into a plate or glass on the serving-table, in case there should be any cork dust in it.

If a gentleman is dining alone at a restaurant, instead of serving him, it is better to place the dishes and wine on the table in front and let him help himself as he wishes.

# CHAPTER 10

# TEA

The Tea, or 'Afternoon Tea' of England, is also becoming every day more in vogue among the aristocracy of all the countries of Europe, and in both Americas.

As is well known, tea is served in England in various ways, according to where and to whom served.

## TEA IN PRIVATE HOUSES

In most private houses in England when tea is taken *en famille*, that is, without special visitors or ceremony, it is served in the dining-room at the same table where the other meals are taken.

According to the number of persons present at this meal, one or more plates of cut bread and butter, on paper d'oyley, are placed on the table; also, some plates of cut cake, various kinds of pastry specially for tea, plates of water-cress, celery, etc., and jam or marmalade.

To the left of the lady of the house are placed as many cups and saucers as persons present at table; and to the right a tray holding a large tea-pot with the tea ready prepared and a jug of boiling water or a silver kettle on a spirit-stand, a jug of cold milk and another (smaller) with cream.

The sugar-basin should be placed on the cloth to the right and a slop-basin on the tray.

The lady of the house generally pours out the tea, and when pouring it she usually asks each person to be served (if she does not already know) 'Do you take sugar?' 'Do you like your tea sweet?'

It is generally the custom to take two cups of tea, and each person helps himself to the things on the table.

Buttered toast, toasted tea cake, muffins, crumpets, etc., are also served at tea.

Tea is not considered as a meal in the proper sense of the word; but only a collation or *tente-en-pié* between luncheon and dinner.

Formerly, tea in private houses was always served on the point of five o'clock; hence the origin of the phrase 'five o'clock tea' used abroad.

## THE WORKING-CLASS TEA

The tea of the English working-class is the most eccentric of meals, and one of the greatest injuries a gourmet could possibly conceive (according to the ideas of Brillat-Savarin); for with the tea they partake of various kinds of salted meat and dried fish, such as 'corned-beef', kippers, bloaters, red herrings, winkles, shrimps, pickles, watercresses, cucumber, lettuce, jam or marmalade, bread and butter, and cake. This incongruous kind of food may, no doubt, be quite nice and tasty for this class of people, but it must shock any one endowed with refined epicurean instinct.

## THE CHILDREN'S TEA

In a family where there is a nursery of small children, tea for them takes the place of dinner or supper. In addition to bread and butter, etc., boiled eggs, some fish, or light meat and fruit are served. This is also called 'High tea' or 'Meat tea.'

## THE DRAWING-ROOM TEA

In a house where the lady receives her intimate friends once a week, tea on this occasion is served in the drawing-room. This is called the 'weekly at-home tea.'

The following is the method of serving tea in the drawing-room: At four o'clock the butler sets ready in the dining-room a large silver tray with all the necessary things, such as cups and saucers, small plates, a slop-basin, two small jugs, one filled with milk, the other with cream, a sugar-basin filled with lump sugar, etc. When the lady rings to order tea, if there are no small appropriate tables in the drawing-room on which to serve it, two small tables must be carried in and covered with tea-cloths. The tea is then made, and the tea-pot with a kettle containing boiling water placed on the tray with the cups, etc., is carried to one of the small tables in the drawing-room and left there. Another tray is then carried in containing plates of finely cut bread and butter, different kinds of cakes, pastries, biscuits, fancy sandwiches of different kinds, etc. (all these are prepared beforehand). The servant then retires, leaving the lady of the house and her daughters (if any) to serve the guests.

## THE RECEPTION TEA

In English high-class society when an 'At-home tea' is given, the service of this is much more elaborate. The number of visitors is sometimes from about eighty to one hundred, and consequently tea is served from a *buffet* in the dining-room or in one of the reception-rooms.

The tables which form the buffet must be raised in height by placing the feet on special blocks.

The buffet tablecloth should reach the carpet and the corners be pinned so as to present a perfectly neat appearance.

Smilax may be used for decoration.

On the buffet are placed (with symmetry and good taste) a selection of sandwiches made with cucumbers, water-cresses, anchovy paste, foie gras, caviare, etc., cut bread and butter, various kinds of cakes, a good assortment of pastries, biscuits and various fruit stands with strawberries or any other fresh fruit in season.

It is scarcely necessary to mention that a large number of plates and forks must be kept on the buffet in readiness; also a large number of cups and saucers for tea and coffee, so as to ensure a rapid and efficient service.

In the centre and on both sides of the *buffet* tall flower-stands should be placed, and in the centre towards the back two large silver urns, one with freshly made coffee and the other with boiling water for making tea.

Besides tea and coffee it is usual at this kind of reception to serve different kinds of ices, in special frosted glass plates, or in paper *caisses*; also champagne and claret cup, jellies and blanc-mange.

Besides the *buffet* there should also be a few small tables about the room, each with a flower-stand upon it, as so many ladies prefer to take tea seated.

For good and efficient service at an 'At-home tea' of this kind, two waiters or servants should be in attendance behind the *buffet* to serve the tea and coffee, two others to attend to the small tables, and two more to remove the dirty things and fetch and carry what may be necessary.

## TEA IN THE HOTEL

In hotels, tea is generally served either in the winter garden, the palm-court, or in the *foyer*.

Just before the hour at which tea is usually served, the small tables are covered with an embroidered tea-cloth, and a small flower-stand placed upon each.

Two or three cups and saucers, a small sugar-basin, two or three small knives, and two or three small plates are placed on each table.

When the guests take their places and order tea, the waiter writes the order in his check-book and either fetches it himself or sends his assistant, if he has one.

Besides the tea and hot water, he should bring from the still-room cut bread and butter, cut cake, buttered toasts, and various kinds of sandwiches.

When the guests are ready, the plates must be changed and a large silver tray containing a large assortment of pastries is presented to them, and they help themselves with a special pair of silver tongs placed on the tray for this purpose.

For tea no serviettes or d'oyleys are put out unless the customers ask for them, as is often the case when strawberries and cream are served.

## HOW TO MAKE GOOD TEA

The reproaches of Continental visitors that a cup of good coffee is unattainable in England would seem to be well founded.

These reproaches could also be extended to tea, for except in the very best houses, 'the cup that cheers' is often depressing.

The proportion of tea to water is usually a matter of individual taste. Owing to the various methods of curing the tea and the many varieties and grades grown in different countries, each of which has its own characteristics, the time allowed for drawing must depend upon the kind of tea used.

Ceylon tea is usually allowed five minutes to draw; China and Japan green teas, six minutes; while China Oolongs require from eight to ten minutes to draw properly.

The infused tea leaves should not be allowed to remain in the tea-pot any longer than the time specified for infusion, as otherwise the liquid turns bitter and is no more the wholesome, fragrant cup of tea for real connoisseurs.

Many devices for its better 'brewing' have from time to time been introduced; but the best tea-pots are those that permit the infused leaves to be separated from the liquid after these have been properly infused, thus avoiding the harmful tannin.

The boiling water used plays an important part in the making of good tea or coffee; and a good many people either ignore this, or wilfully overlook this fact.

The water must always be freshly boiled; as water that has been boiling longer than three or four minutes loses in evaporation its natural good properties and is not fit for the purpose of making either tea or coffee. Stale water or water that has boiled for some time is sure to spoil the flavour of the best tea or coffee.

When making tea always rinse the tea-pot first with boiling water; then add the tea and pour in the freshly boiled water; allow the tea the correct time to draw, then take out the leaves and serve.

# CHAPTER II

# DINNER

The decoration and appointments of the table for a ceremonious dinner-party form one of the most important duties of the mistress of the house (or the Maître d'hôtel, as the case may be), for on this occasion the importance of the establishment and the efficiency of its employees are revealed more than on any other.

Whether in a private house, or in a hotel or restaurant, the same general rules have to be observed, and on these depend the orderliness and harmony of the service.

The laying of the table for a special dinner-party should be commenced at about two or three o'clock in the afternoon; for the floral decoration and the many things that have to be prepared beforehand take up a considerable amount of time.

## SERVICE À LA FRANÇAISE

This style originated in the great houses of the old French nobility, who passed the greater part of their time either inviting, or being invited, to sumptuous feasts and trying to rival each other *dans l'art de bien manger.*

The *Service à la Française* consisted (and still consists in some places) in serving the meal in three parts with three different services. Before announcing to the host and hostess that 'dinner was served', the soup was served in the plate of each of the guests. When this was finished and the dirty plates removed, various kinds of *Hors-d'œuvre*, two or three kinds of fish and of meat with the accompanying vegetables or sauces were placed on the table. Altogether this was called the first service.

When this first service was finished, the servants removed the dishes and the dirty plates and brought in the second service, consisting of three or four different roasts with their accompanying vegetables, gravies, sauces and salads.

It was then the custom for the host to carve and serve the guests himself, helped by his servants. For this reason the art of carving at table was considered an honourable distinction.

The third service consisted of various hot sweets such as flans, puddings, tarts, pies, etc., and different kinds of dry and fresh fruit, pastes, cheeses, *compôtes, bon-bons*, etc. All this was put on the table at the same time. This agglomeration of plates, dishes on the *réchauds*, bottles, etc., did not give much room for anything in the way of floral nor any other kind of decoration, except for a massive silver centre-piece.

This style, *à la Française*, was in vogue in private houses all over Europe until it was replaced by the better and more practical service *à la Russe.*

53

Although the service *à la Française* is still preferred by some people who consider that it lends itself better to opulence and display, the service *à la Russe* offers infinitely more advantages, since it allows the guests to partake of the different dishes while they are hot and palatable without the necessity of long delays in the service as was unavoidable in the service *à la Française.*

This style of serving *à la Française* is still adopted by many families of modest means, and more especially in the numerous English 'boarding-houses' where the eternal 'joint of beef or mutton' and 'rabbit pie', and other etceteras, are placed on the table, to be served by the landlady to her paying guests, and form the ever-prevailing dish (*faute de mieux*) of the boarders.

## SERVICE À LA RUSSE

The service *à la Russe* consists in serving the dishes one after the other, 'piping hot' straight from the kitchen, without letting the guests wait for anything.

In Russia, the first part of the dinner is served outside the dining-room; that is, in an ante-chamber close to the entrance to the dining-room, there is a sideboard or small *buffet* containing all kinds of *Hors-d'œuvre à la Russe* and Russian liqueurs, called *Zakuska* and *Vodka,*  also, French and Italian Vermouth, Gin, Madeira, Sherry wine, etc., with the corresponding glasses beside them. About ten or fifteen minutes before dinner the gentlemen help themselves to these at pleasure.

The same kind of *Zakuska* liqueurs, etc., are served on a large silver tray to the ladies in the drawing-room.

---

* Vodka and all grain spirits, by the way, were banned in the Czar's dominions soon after the outbreak of the European War.

The service *à la Russe* does not admit of anything being placed on the centre of the table except the floral decoration, and in no case may any hot dish be placed upon it.

If the dinner is not one of very great *etiquette*, it is permissible to put on the table a *Pâté de foie gras truffé* or a *Galantine de Faisan habillée*, if they are artistically arranged; also a pretty *corbeille* made of sugar filled with bon-bons and *friandises*.

If the dinner is *en famille* it is permissible to put the water jugs and wine decanters on the table; also the fruit in fruit-stands; but in the case of a dinner of *etiquette* in a house of the aristocracy, nothing whatever is put on the centre of the table but the flowers, candlesticks, salt and pepper.

To ensure rapid and efficient service everything required during the meal should be placed beforehand on the sideboards and serving-table, such as large cold plates for cold meat or fowl, salad plates, sweet plates, reserve knives and forks of all kinds, all the requisites for carving, soup spoons, spoons for gravy, glasses for water and liqueurs, reserve bread, butter, ice, English and French mustard, various kinds of sauces (such as A1, Worcestershire Sauce, etc.), cut brown bread and butter and Chili vinegar if there are oysters, lemons cut in four for fried fish, chutney if there is curry, currant jelly if there is roast mutton or venison, dry biscuits and celery if there is cheese to be served, etc., etc.

In addition, fruit plates must be prepared, each with their corresponding white d'oyleys, glass finger-bowl and silver fruit knife and fork.

The water for the finger-bowls should be slightly warmed in winter, but as cool as possible in summer.

In houses and hotels *de luxe* it is customary to put just a dash of rose-water or a slice of lemon into the finger-bowls.

The fruit plates thus prepared and the coffee service should be placed on a sideboard, or on a table in a convenient corner of the dining-room, or, if there is no space, in an adjacent room.

At the majority of dinner-parties such dishes as salmon, turbot, joints of mutton or veal, capons, etc., are sent up whole, and it is the duty of the Maître d'hôtel (or butler if in a private house) to carve these in the correct fashion, as explained in Chapter 22.

Before beginning to carve a joint, it is presented to the host (this in hotels and restaurants only) at his left side for his notice and approval.

If everything is properly prepared beforehand, a dinner of twelve or fourteen covers can easily be served, in the dining-room, by two waiters and an extra butler to serve the wines and liqueurs. If the kitchen and pantry are far away from the dining-room, it is always better to have a young assistant to help carry the dishes, etc.

In a private house it could be arranged to have two servants (men or women) in the dining-room, two more to fetch and carry the dishes and plates, and the butler to direct the service and serve the wines, etc. At a dinner of *etiquette* it is the custom for the waiters or servants always to wear white gloves, white ties, and white waistcoats.

A full dinner, modern style, consists of the following courses: I.—*Hors-d'œuvre variés* (or oysters or caviare); II.—Two soups (one thick and one clear); III.—Two kinds of fish (one large boiled, the other small fried); IV.—An *entrée*; V.—The joint or *pièce de résistance*; VI.—The sorbet; VII.—The roast and salad; VIII.—A dish of vegetables; IX.—A hot sweet; X.—An ice-cream and wafers; XI.— Dessert (fresh and dry fruits); XII.—The coffee and liqueurs.

## MENU

| | |
|---|---|
| *Caviar d'Esterlet Rafraîchi* | Cold Caviare |
| *Hors-d'œuvre Variés* | Appetisers |
| | |
| *Consommé Prince de Galles* | Clear Soup Prince of Wales |
| *Crème Favorite* | Chicken and Cream Soup |
| | |
| *Saumon Bouilli, Sauce Victoria* | Boiled Salmon, Lobster Sauce |
| *Salade de Concombres* | Cucumber Salad |
| | |
| *Buisson de Filets de Soles* | Very small fried |
| *en Goujons* | Fillets of Sole |
| | |
| *Selle de Venaison Grand Veneur* | Saddle of Venison |
| *Purée de Marrons* | Chestnut Purée |
| *Pommes Dauphine* | Dauphine Potatoes |
| | |
| *Timbale de Cailles Souvaroff* | Quails Souvaroff |
| | |
| *Granité au Champagne* | Champagne Sherbet |
| *Cigarettes Russes* | Russian Cigarettes |
| | |
| *Chapon à la Broche* | Roast Capon |
| *Salade de Cœurs de Laitue* | Lettuce Hearts Salad |
| | |
| *Asperges d'Argenteuil* | Large French Asparagus |
| *Sauce Divine et Beurre Fondu* | Divine Sauce and Melted Butter |
| | |
| *Pudding Diplomate* | Diplomat Pudding |
| | |
| *Fraises Sarah-Bernhardt* | Strawberries Sarah-Bernhardt |
| *Petits Fours et Friandises* | Petits Fours and Friandises |
| | |
| *Dessert* | Dessert |
| | |
| *Café et Liqueurs* | Coffee and Liqueurs |

As is well known, the best wines, the best cooks and cooking come from France; so, it is not therefore a matter for surprise, even in this country, to see the menus written in French.

The menu on the previous page may be taken as a fair sample for a complete good dinner.

This menu, of course, may be enlarged or diminished according to the occasion, and I insert it merely to give a general idea.

Let me now, dear reader, take you step by step through all the courses of a complete dinner and tell you exactly how every course should be served. If you already know, skip it, and proceed to the next chapter.

Immediately after the guests are seated, the *Hors-d'œuvre* are served. As is well known, these consist of sardines in oil or *à la tomate*, anchovies, salamis, radishes, olives, Russian and other salads, smoked salmon, smoked ham, oysters, caviare, pheasant and plovers' eggs, melon, and endless variety of *canapés* with appetising tit-bits.

The ordinary *Hors-d'œuvre* are served on a special dish, or in long small dishes on a stand, or placed on a silver tray with a napkin to prevent sliding. Care must be taken in serving these to begin with the lady on the right of the host and to finish with the host himself. A second waiter should follow the first to hand butter and toasts.

Caviare is served very cold, either in the jar itself or in a silver timbale placed on crushed ice. A dessertspoonful is the proper quantity for a guest.

The correct way to serve caviare is on *blinis* (a kind of thin buttered crumpet) or on a round of hot buttered toast. Some gourmets eat the caviare plain with bread and butter; but others prefer to season it with pepper and lemon juice, or chopped raw onions.

Oysters are served opened in their deep shell, placed on crushed ice on a large silver dish with little *bouquets* of parsley, and half a small lemon for each guest.

The dish of oysters may be handed round for the guests to help themselves to as many as they please; but it is much more practical to place four or six on each plate on the service table.

With oysters, cut brown bread and butter is served; also cut lemon or Chili vinegar, *mignonette* (crushed corn-pepper) and horse-radish powder.

If any of the guests do not take oysters, they should be handed immediately the *Hors-d'œuvre*, so as to keep company with the others.

When each guest has been helped to oysters the wine-butler hands round the chablis, commencing with the lady seated at the right-hand side of the host.

Melon must be served very cold and should be brought into the dining-room cut in slices and placed on crushed ice in a silver dish. To ensure that the slices stand up properly, a small piece of the rind should be cut from the middle.

With the melon, castor sugar and powdered ginger are served, handed on a plate with a folded serviette.

As soon as the *Hors-d'œuvre* are served, the soup should be sent for.

Let me here emphasise that all dishes, gravies, sauces, etc., must be handed at the guest's left side. Plates also are removed and replaced from the left, unless a guest is sitting near a wall or pillar and so renders this impossible. Bread, sugar and coffee are also handed at the left hand. The only things served at the right hand are wines, liqueurs, the tea-pots, the water, and ice in the glasses.

When a dinner is served *à la Russe*, the soup must not be placed on the table before dinner is announced as is the case with the service *à la Française*.

The two soup-tureens are placed on the *réchaud* on the serving table with a pile of hot soup plates before each. According to circumstances the soup is served by the Maître d'hôtel, the butler, or any other servant, with another to carry the plates to the guests (a plate of each kind of soup in either hand), taking care to ask in a low voice 'Clear or thick soup?' and to serve the one preferred.

The soup plates are placed on a flat plate, which the waiter takes in his hand.

At this point the wine-butler pours out the Sherry.

As soon as the soup is served the fish must be ordered, and when this is served, the next course must be ordered, and so on successively throughout the meal.

Whoever is responsible for the service should see that there are no delays, and on the other hand that the dishes are not sent too soon to the dining-room, but must be arranged so that each course is served hot immediately on leaving the kitchen.

In private houses the butler informs the cook by means of an electric bell when the next course is to be sent up.

The dirty plates of each course should not be removed from the table until nearly all the guests have finished eating.

The butler responsible for serving the wines should observe the method described in Chapters 25 and 26.

Fish.—When this is a whole salmon or turbot, the dish is first presented to the host, with the cover raised at his left side; this is then placed on the *réchaud* and carved and served in the manner explained in Chapter 22.

If two kinds of fish are served the second is either whitebait, smelts, or fillets of soles cut in the shape of whitebait and fried.

Small lemons cut in two, and cut brown bread and butter, are also handed round with this service.

ENTRÉE.—The entrée or dish following the fish (in England) is served in the dish just as it is sent from the kitchen and is passed round to the guests in the order described in Chapter 5.

The entrée consists generally of jointed braised fowls, salmis of game, quails or anything of the kind that needs no carving in the dining-room.

THE JOINT.—The joint follows the entrée; and may be either a leg, shoulder, or saddle of lamb, or mutton or venison, a York ham, a *fricandeau de veau*, a larded whole fillet of beef, or the familiar roast-beef. Two or three green vegetables and potatoes are invariably served with the joint.

After it has been presented before the host, it is placed on the *réchaud* on the service table to be carved by the butler or the Maître d'hôtel (according to where the dinner is served). The slices should be cut in portions large enough for each guest, and when placed on the hot meat plates are handed immediately. One or two more waiters pass round the corresponding gravies or sauces and vegetables.

THE SORBET.—The sorbet is served in small cut glasses for this purpose. They are sent into the room on a silver tray, and on the service table are placed each on a small plate with its corresponding teaspoon, before serving them to the guests.

As soon as the sorbet is served, the butler or a waiter hands round a large box of Russian cigarettes, and a second one passes a lighted spirit lamp or a small candle.

After a few minutes pause, the sorbet is followed by the—

ROAST.—If the roast consists of quails, snipes, or any other dish not requiring carving, this is passed round as explained for the entrée; but should it be capons or poulardes, turkeys or ducks, they are sent in whole, and after being carved are handed round on the dish, accompanied by the gravy and salad; the latter is served on half-moon shaped plates.

NOTE.—With roast turkey, it is customary to serve cranberry sauce; with roast-beef, Yorkshire pudding and horse-radish sauce; with roast lamb, mint sauce; with roast mutton and venison, red-currant jelly; with roast pork and roast goose, apple sauce; with pheasant, chicken or grouse, bread sauce and bread-crumbs; with salmon, cucumber salad; with all kinds of fried fish, cut lemons; with whitebait, cut bread and butter, and cayenne pepper; with turtle soup, Madeira wine or milk-punch and cut lemon; and with all curried dishes, chutney and Bombay ducks.

VEGETABLES.—The vegetables are better handed straight away in the same dish as they come from the kitchen. When there are green peas or spinach with cream, only a spoon need be put in the dish to serve them round. Asparagus may also be handed round, but it is better to serve them on the plates on the serving table, the sauces only being handed round.

PUDDING.—The pudding, or other sweets, may be handed round or served on the service table according to their nature and the most convenient way of serving them; the object being to provide the greatest comfort and pleasure to the guests. There are many sweet dishes that are not only difficult to hand round for the guests to help themselves, but at a large table almost impossible, owing to the risk involved to the guests' dresses in so doing.

For instance, a large *omelette en surprise*, a large cherry tart, or a large bombe of ice-cream dressed on a heavy block of carved ice, is better served on the service table on the guests' plates and these handed round.

Ice.—The ice-cream is always accompanied by wafers, *petits fours* or *friandises*, which are handed round. After the ice comes the—

Savoury.—With this service, as with the dessert, special decanted fine Bordeaux and old Port-wine are served, and it is customary when all the guests have been served by the butler to place the bottles on the table in front of the host, who then refills the glasses of his immediate friends. The butler must have the corresponding glasses ready on a silver tray to hand them round when required.

Cheese.—Cheese is almost invariably served at luncheon, but seldom, if ever, at dinner-time. When cheese is served at luncheon it should be accompanied by dry biscuits, celery (if in season), and fresh butter.

Dessert.—Before serving the dessert, all cruets, empty bottles and glasses, spare silver, etc., must be removed and the breadcrumbs brushed off the table. As soon as the dessert plates with the finger-bowls are placed round the table, the fruit is handed round to the guests just as it is on the dishes, except in the case of bananas and grapes, the former being cut off singly and the latter into small bunches, before being handed round.

Pine-apples, also, are peeled and cut into slices on the service table, previous to serving them.

After handing the fruit round, the fruit dishes should be placed on the table, and the waiters retire from the room.

Coffee.—The coffee and liqueurs are not always served at the dinner-table. In most private houses, when the dessert is over, the hostess either nods or smiles at the lady at the right of her husband and rises; the rest of the ladies do the same and follow her to the drawing-room, where they are rejoined by the gentlemen about half an hour later.

During this half-hour or so, the gentlemen remain in the dining-room; they draw close to the host, and finish their wine, or drink coffee and smoke, while one of them, perhaps, tells an after-dinner short story.

The ladies take coffee in the drawing-room; the butler, assisted by the footmen, carries in the coffee cups three parts filled on a large silver tray; and in the centre of the tray are placed a sugar basin, a jug of cream and another with hot milk.

The coffee thus may be handed round to each lady, or may be left on a convenient table for the ladies to help themselves. Coffee is served in the same way to the gentlemen.

When the coffee is served on the dining-table to all the guests together, a coffee cup and saucer with the corresponding spoon placed on a plate of the same service is put before each guest; one waiter hands round the sugar and another pours out the coffee and milk or cream.

When the party is entertained in a fashionable hotel or restaurant, and the coffee and liqueurs are not taken at the dining-table, these are served in the palm-court, the *foyer*, or the winter-garden of the establishment.

NOTE.—The dinner-table arrangements and the waiting at table explained above are much about the same whether the dinner is given in a private house or at a hotel or restaurant.

It is almost unnecessary to say that whilst waiting at table the movements of the waiters or servants should be quiet and natural. A waiter who bustles or runs in and out of the dining-room during the dinner for no particular purpose, and when taking up or putting down plates on the service table makes unnecessary noise or clatter, shows his inefficiency and cannot do otherwise than cause displeasure to the party. A waiter never knows his business too well; and if he wishes to succeed, now that he has the opportunity, he should acquire a thorough knowledge of his profession, so as to act intelligently in the performance of all his duties.

When it happens that two ordinary servants or waiters have to serve a dinner with a butler or Maître d'hôtel to direct the service, they should have a thorough understanding before the dinner begins as to the part each is going to play or the side each is going to serve, so as to do the waiting diligently without undue haste or delay, and above all in a perfectly noiseless manner.

The one who acts as *commis*, or runner, brings the dishes and hot plates from the kitchen into the dining-room, and places them on the *réchaud* or hot-plate. He must see that all the plates are well polished and that there is the same number as guests at table. Whenever there is a chicken, duck, or sirloin steak to carve, he must not forget to bring an extra plate for that purpose, for he who is deficient in memory has to go back and make up for the deficiency with his legs.

The *commis* should never leave the room empty-handed. During dinner there are always dirty plates, empty dishes, and countless other things on the service table waiting to be cleared away, and there is nothing like clearing away as one goes.

The *chef de rang* or table waiter should never leave the dining-room during dinner, as he must be ever watchful over the service and the wants of the guests.

The *commis* must make a point of always being in the room ready by the table, when it is time to hand round the sauces, gravies, vegetables or salads, and to make himself thoroughly useful.

## HOW TO MAKE GOOD FRENCH COFFEE

France is the country where coffee forms the regular after-meals drink of the people, and where the art of 'Coffee-making' is

65

thoroughly understood. The coffee beans must be skilfully roasted the same day and ground just before using.

Mocha and Caracolillo coffee in equal parts form an ideal blend: Mocha is a strong full-bodied coffee, but possesses little aroma; Caracolillo coffee is just the reverse; but the happy union of the two makes a delicious after-dinner coffee for real epicures.

For every small cup of black coffee, a dessertspoonful of ground coffee (not pulverised) is required; for half a large breakfast cup a large tablespoonful. The breakfast *café au lait* is usually served half milk and half coffee.

The freshly boiled water must be at full boiling point before pouring it on the coffee in the coffee machine.

Coffee should never boil, as it loses its fine aroma, becomes bitter to the taste, and is unwholesome to drink.

NOTE.—On making either tea or coffee it is required to allow an extra cup for the pot.

### HOW TO MAKE TURKISH COFFEE

Turkish coffee is most delicious after dinner, and is becoming more in favour every day amongst the well-to-do people. This accounts, perhaps, for the fashionable hotels and restaurants keeping a native of Turkey, attired in his gorgeous national costume, specially to make and serve this beverage.

I am indebted to Messrs. J. Picard & Co., 'Specialists in patent cafetières and coffee', of Planter's Hall, 117, Regent Street, W., for the following directions for making good Turkish coffee:

'Fill the cafetière three-quarters full with water and allow the water to just reach boiling point whilst on the spirit lamp. Withdraw, and then put the coffee (*very finely ground*) into the cafetière, with sugar as desired, and stir. Replace the cafetière on the spirit lamp over a medium flame; the moment the whole reaches boiling point, the liquid will rise in the same way as boiling milk does; then instantly withdraw. Repeat this twice (in all three times); allow the grounds to sink to the bottom of the vessel and serve.

'A few drops of cold water sprinkled on the coffee will make the grounds sink quickly, but it is preferable to await the settling of the grounds, and thus retain all the froth.

'The ordinary allowance is a teaspoonful of finely ground coffee to every Turkish cup, or two to a demi-tasse. A very small piece of lemon or vanilla is sometimes added according to taste.'

# CHAPTER 12

# SUPPER

In the houses of the upper classes where the principal meal is generally served between seven and eight o'clock in the evening, supper is not served unless there is a ball or a reception.

In London, supper is served only in the restaurants to people 'du grand monde' after the theatre between eleven and half-past twelve at night; and also in the clubs, where, as it is known, suppers are served until two in the morning.

In Paris, Berlin, Vienna, and Buenos Aires, the restaurants are not obliged to close at midnight or half-past twelve, as is the case in London; consequently suppers, etc., last practically all night.

Supper in a restaurant may consist of one or two courses *à la carte* according to the pleasure of the guest.

In the *restaurants de luxe* 'set suppers' at a fixed price are generally served.

*Consommé Riche en Tasse (Chaud, Froid et en Gelée)*

*Pilaw de Homard à la Turque*

*Côtelettes d'Agneau aux Pointes d'Asperges*
*Pommes Anna*

*Cailles à la Richelieu*

*Buffet Froid*
*Salade Rachel*

*Terrine de Foie Gras Truffé*

*Pêches Melba*
*Friandises*

The preceding is a specimen supper menu as served at fashionable restaurants.

When the set supper is not taken, the customers requiring just a 'snack', each usually chooses from the *carte* either two devilled kidneys, two lamb cutlets from the grill, one veal cutlet, or a grilled chicken and bacon (if a party of three or four) with the corresponding vegetables or salad.

Often they are satisfied either with half a lobster, a slice of galantine and cold ham, or even with a Welsh rare-bit.

The method of waiting at table and serving suppers is much the same as already explained for luncheon or dinner.

The service and arrangements for a large ball-supper are more elaborate and are explained in detail in Chapter 17.

# CHAPTER 13

# ANCIENT AND MODERN
# BANQUETS

Although now-a-days everybody has more or less an idea of what a banquet is, this book can hardly be considered as complete without mentioning these special functions.

The word 'banquet' is synonymous with 'feast', which was the name given in olden times to the pompous dinners and their accompanying orgies, such as those given by the defender of Babylon to his nobles and courtiers.

Amongst the magnificence and splendours of the palace of Lucullus, the Roman General, mention is made of the various sumptuous banqueting-halls named after different gods and planets.

According to legend, these feasts of Lucullus varied greatly in nature; and for each kind of feast a special banqueting hall was assigned; so that he had only to mention the name of a certain hall, such as 'Bacchus', 'Cupid', or 'Venus', etc., and his servants knew immediately and perfectly what they had to prepare for the feast in question.

On one occasion Cicero and Pompey tried to catch him unawares, but they, themselves, were surprised at the majestic banquet with which they were regaled, in spite of the fact that Lucullus gave no orders at all to his servants, but merely indicated that he wished to be served in the 'Apollo' Hall.

Lucullus was renowned for his epicurean tastes and for the luxury and wealth he displayed. To give an idea of this, it is said that once when he was dining alone and his Maître d'hôtel did not serve him with the usual splendour, he remarked in a haughty manner: 'Did you not know that Lucullus was to-day dining at Lucullus' palace?'

The magnificence of the Emperor Nero in this respect excelled that of all his contemporaries. In his palace called 'The Golden House', so named because it was covered outside and in with gold and ornamented with diamonds and pearls, he had the roof of one of its magnificent halls made to imitate the firmament in motion, revolving day and night, and changing in scene during the meals as the different dishes were placed on the table.

By means of springs the servants could at will make a fine rain of perfumed water fall lightly down on the assembled guests.

To characterise his extravagant ostentation, Nero's *ragoût* of nightingales' tongues is often mentioned when a modern epicure has too fastidious tastes.

Such ostentatious banquets as those were doubtless in vogue in those days; but nothing of this kind is seen now, except perhaps, with the exception of once a year, in the London Guildhall, when the Lord Mayor's Banquet takes place on the 9th of November, and once in every ten years in the *Galerie des Machines* at the International Paris Exhibition. This banquet consists of 20,000 covers, served in honour of the Mayors of France, who are all assembled together for the occasion at the same table.

## MODERN BANQUETS

The manner of constructing the tables for an ordinary banquet depends, of course, on the number of diners and the shape or form of the hall in which the banquet is given. If the guests number from fifty to one hundred, the table is generally in the form of a T or U unless the guests prefer to be seated at small separate tables as in a restaurant.

When the number of guests amounts to several hundred, the most practical shape arrangement of the tables is that called the *peigne*, which consists in one long table the whole length of the hall opposite the entrance, and various others joined to this at intervals of two and a half yards, the whole resembling a comb (*peigne*) in shape.

It has already been stated in a preceding chapter that the height of the banquet or dining-room tables should be 28 inches and the distance between the centres of each cover from 24 to 30 inches.

The arrangement of the covers, candlesticks, salt-cellars, etc., is more or less the same as at the *Table d'hôte*. The flowers are arranged in small vases or are disposed on the tablecloth in some pretty design, in combination with the smilax which trails over the cloth.

According to the importance of the banquet each waiter attends to six, eight, or ten guests.

The wine-butlers serve the wines, mineral waters, liqueurs, and cigars; and each waits on from twenty to twenty-five guests.

The method of serving the wine is fully explained in Chapter 25.

When waiting at a banquet, each waiter should begin to hand the *Hors-d'œuvre* to the first guest seated on the left of his own party and go on in succession till the end. With the soup or next course, he should start with the first guest on the right, and so on successively till the end of the dinner, no precedence being given on these occasions to rank or sex.

As soon as the coffee is served, all the waiters, with the exception of those serving the wine, leave the banqueting-room and wash up the glasses and put everything (or as much as possible) in order. The wine-butlers, who remain until the end, serve wine, liqueurs, cigars, etc., as they are asked.

While the chairman or other guest is speaking, the waiters should refrain from going to and fro or making any noise.

Before leaving the hall at the end of dinner each waiter should leave his own sideboard or serving-table perfectly clear of both clean and dirty plates and silver.

# CHAPTER 14

# THE LORD MAYOR'S BANQUET

The Lord Mayor's Show and the Lord Mayor's Banquet constitute a London National *fête*. This banquet is a relic of the ancient splendour of the English nobility. Any one entering the Guildhall for the first time while the Lord Mayor's Banquet is taking place could not be otherwise than overwhelmed, for the *éclat* and the buzz of animated conversation of the thousand and some odd guests (not to mention the waiters), the noise of the service, the music and the general clamour are indescribable.

The great historic hall, illumined with thousands of electric lights during the banquet, forms an imposing spectacle.

After the Civic Pageant has passed through the City and part of the West End, forming one of the most picturesque sights seen in the London streets, the Lord Mayor and Lady Mayoress receive their guests in state in a remarkably brilliant reception room.

They afterwards enter the Great Hall where the Banquet takes place, the Lord Mayor leading with the Prime Minister's wife. He takes the place of honour at the centre of the table seated in a gilt arm-chair. He is arrayed in his robes of state with a large gold chain round his neck and his breast covered with various decorations.

To his right and left are seated every one of eminence in the land; the Ministers of the Crown, the Lord Chief Justice, the Ambassadors from all the diplomatic bodies in London, all wearing their state dress, and when the banquet is concluded make speeches referring to the politics of the day.

To the right and left on a platform opposite the principal entrance may be seen half a dozen or more stalwart cooks and carvers resplendent in their caps, coats, and aprons white as snow, knife and fork in hand, carving with the utmost skill and rapidity the famous 'Baron of beef.'

At either extremity of the Great Hall stand the trumpeters in their white wigs and magnificent scarlet livery profusely embellished with gold, blowing flourishes on their trumpets answering one another across the Great Hall like the echo between two mountains.

On a little platform behind the Lord Mayor stands the 'toast master' conspicuously attired in quaint robes announcing in sonorous powerful voice the orders of his 'master' and the different toasts of the banquet.

The whole is a scene of utmost splendour and brilliancy and imposing in the extreme.

The average cost of the Lord Mayor's Banquet is £2,000 or about £2 2s. per head. The menu cards, printed in English, are worthy of the occasion.

The following are typical menus:

# NOVEMBER 9

## WINES

Punch

———

SHERRY
Gonzalez-Byass

———

HOCK
Rudisheim

———

CHAMPAGNE
Cliquot, 1904
Bollinger, 1904

———

MOSELLE
Scharzberger

———

CLARET
Château La Rose, 1899

———

PORT WINE
Dow's, 1896

———

LIQUEURS
Bénédictine
Grande Chartreuse

———

MINERALS
Perrier water

## MENU

TURTLE
Clear Turtle

———

Fillets of Turbot *Dugléré*

———

Mousses of Lobster Cardinal

———

Sweetbread and Truffles

———

Baron of Beef
Salads

———

Partridges

———

Mutton Cutlets Royale

———

Smoked Tongue

———

Orange Jelly

———

Italian Creams

———

Strawberry Creams
Maids of Honour

———

*Pâtisserie Princesse*
Meringues

'An ideal and carefully thought-out menu', said a London doctor to a representative of the Press on this occasion.

# THE LORD MAYOR'S BANQUET

| WINES | MENU |
|---|---|
| **SHERRY** | **TURTLE** |
| Amontillado | Clear Turtle |
| | |
| **CHAMPAGNE** | Fried Fillets of Soles |
| Clicquot, 1906 | Tartare Sauce |
| Bollinger, 1906 | |
| Roederer, 1906 | Mutton Cutlets Royale |
| | |
| **CLARET** | Baron of Beef. Salads |
| Château La Rose, 1899 | |
| | Casserole of Pheasant |
| **PORT WINE** | |
| Gonzalez's Old Portugal | Smoked Tongue |
| | |
| **BRANDY** | Orange Jelly |
| Denis Monnié, 1865 | Charlotte Russe |
| | Creams |
| Schweppes' Malvern | Bavarois |
| and Soda Waters | Meringues |
| | Maids of Honour |
| | *Petits Gateaux* |
| | |
| | Ice |
| | |
| | Dessert |

The menu cards for 1914 bore a specially pretty design in colours, representing the intertwined flags of the allied nations at war.

The catering of these renowned banquets is carried out in excellent style by Messrs. Ring & Brymer.

# CHAPTER 15

# WEDDING LUNCHEONS

When a large number of guests are invited to a really smart Wedding Luncheon, the hour is between two and three o'clock and is generally given at a good hotel on account of the greater facilities.

If the wedding is a quiet or a small one, then, the lunch or whatever refreshment is given after the ceremony takes place at the bride's parents' house.

When only light refreshments are offered, it is a stand-up affair, and a *buffet* is set out either in the dining-room or some other convenient place according to the space at disposal or other circumstances.

Light refreshments may in this case consist of hot or cold consommé in cups, assorted sandwiches, pastries, jellies, blanc-mange, etc., various wines, claret cup, lemonade, ices, tea, coffee, etc.

When a proper sit-down luncheon is given, it is served in the dining-room.

This luncheon is served in much the same way as any ordinary luncheon (or breakfast if the ceremony takes place in the morning); the only difference being the extra dishes, the profusion of white flowers, the speeches, and the prevailing excitement of the guests.

The arrangement of the tables for a sit-down luncheon must be made according to the size of the room and number of guests. There may be one large table in the centre, or a number of small tables to seat either four, six or eight guests. In either case there must be a *table d'honneur* in a selected part of the room for the bride and bridegroom, the parents of both, the 'Best-man', the Bridesmaids, and a few of the principal guests.

The way to lay the table for a wedding luncheon as far as plates, silver and glasses are concerned also is much the same as for any other special occasion; the only difference being that the wedding cake and the bride's bouquet must be placed in the centre of the table in front of the newly wedded couple; the flowers must also be white (*de rigueur*) and choice; the menu, printed as a rule in silver on dainty and appropriate menu cards or on white satin, is placed on silver menu holders, or against the champagne glasses, or laid flat on the left side of each guest's place.

Very frequently silver cups and ornaments belonging to the family, or relations of the *nouveaux mariés*, are used for the decoration of the table.

Bronze statuettes representing cupids armed with bow and arrow, small silver cardboard horseshoes, and sometimes rich confetti are also used for the embellishment of the table.

To ensure good service, each waiter should not wait on more than four or six persons. They should wear the usual dress-coat with white waistcoat, white tie and white cotton gloves.

When a *fête* of this kind takes place at a hotel, as is frequently the case among well-to-do people, the luncheon is served in one of the special *salons* for this purpose. The charge per head may be from ten shillings up to ten pounds according to the choice and amount of wines, flowers, food and the band supplied.

In the case of a stand-up luncheon with only light refreshments, the charge per head is much reduced, but on the other hand the number of guests is generally much greater.

The arrangements for the serving of a stand-up wedding luncheon are very simple. A long *buffet* is set up at the end of the room about a yard and a half from the wall. The tablecloth should just touch the carpet in front, and at the back should hang a few inches only.

Two large silver urns, one containing boiling water to make tea when required, and the other with freshly made coffee, are placed one on either side of the *buffet*.

Garlands of smilax and very high flower-vases are used to decorate the *buffet*.

The wedding-cake is placed either in the centre of the buffet, or on a table by itself in the middle of the room.

All the good things to be offered to the guests should be placed on the *buffet* just a few minutes before their arrival, so that everything may be fresh and appetising.

Along the front of the *buffet* must be placed as many covers as possible, close together, consisting of one small plate, one small steel knife and fork, a dessert-spoon, two glasses, one for Port wine and the other for Champagne. A good supply of cups for *consommé* (if figuring on the menu), tea and coffee, and sugar-basins must be placed ready on a sideboard standing between the wall and the *buffet*; also small plates, silver, glasses, and fruit plates with their corresponding d'oyleys and finger-bowls.

Two waiters must be posted behind the *buffet* to serve and hand over cups of *consommé*, tea or coffee, ices, and everything required by the guests, and two others at the front of the *buffet* to replace the emptied dishes, to remove dirty plates, glasses, etc. They must also relay the covers and supply everything required throughout the function.

At these functions the waiters do not actually wait, for as a rule the gentlemen wait on the ladies and then help themselves.

In addition to the *buffet* there should be a number of small fancy tables, nicely laid out, placed about the same room and outside for the use of those guests who prefer to have a sit-down *tête-à-tête*.

These tables should be attended by other waiters and must contain an assortment of tempting delicacies. Gentlemen sitting at these tables, however, will go up to the *buffet* and choose what each thinks acceptable to his lady companion.

At all smart weddings, the bride and bridegroom's presents are on view in an adjacent room; this room is prepared and decorated a day or two before and arranged with several tables round covered with green baize or white cloth, on which the wedding presents are displayed.

When a sit-down luncheon is given, the table is arranged in the same way as for a banquet, and everything is, of course, on a much larger scale than when given in a private house, as already explained.

## MENU

| | |
|---|---|
| *Canapés au Caviar* | Caviare on Toasts |
| *Consommé à la Royale* | Consommé Royal |
| *Crème Reine Margot* | Cream Soup Queen Margot |
| *Mayonnaise de Homard* | Lobster Mayonnaise |
| *Filets de Soles Bagration* | Fillets of Soles Bagration |
| *Côtelettes d'Agneau* | Lamb Cutlets and Asparagus |
| *aux Pointes d'Asperges* | Points |
| *Pommes Parisiennes* | Parisian Potatoes |
| *Poularde au Riz,* | Fowl with Rice, |
| *Sauce Suprême* | Supreme Sauce |
| *Pâté de Gibier à la Strassbourg* | Truffled Game Pie |
| *Cailles Richelieu en Gelée* | Cold Quails Richelieu |
| *Janettes de Volaille* | Cold Fowl in Jelly |
| *Pâté de Foie Gras Truffé* | Truffled Pâté of Foie Gras |
| *Jambon d'York* | Cold Ham |
| *Langue Écarlate* | Ecarlate Tongue |
| *Salade de Saison* | Salad |
| *Macédoine de Fruits* | Fruit Salad |
| *aux Liqueurs* | with Liqueurs |
| *Meringues à la Chantilly* | Chantilly Meringues |
| *Gelée à l'Orange* | Orange Jelly |
| *Mousses aux Fraises* | Strawberry Mousse |
| *Rochers de Glaces assortis* | Assorted Ices |
| *Petits-fours. Friandises* | Fancy Cakes |
| *Dessert* | Dessert |
| *Gâteau de Noces* | Wedding Cake |
| *Café et Liqueurs* | Coffee and Liqueurs |

The menu shown on the preceding page is a fair specimen of what may be expected at a wedding luncheon at a good hotel.

The bride always cuts the first slice of cake, which is partaken of after the actual meal is finished. The cake is cut with a large silver knife for that purpose; but this being a rather hard task, the icing being somewhat difficult to cut through, it is generally considered sufficient if she only makes the first incision.

Large wedding cakes are, as a rule, sent out with a large wedge already cut through and fastened round with a white silk ribbon.

The wedge of cake is usually cut up into small long pieces by the Maître d'hôtel (these pieces should each consist of icing and cake) and then handed round on a small silver tray or on dessert plates, to all the guests present.

# CHAPTER 16

# WEDDING RECEPTIONS

When one sees an awning up and a crimson carpet laid on the front steps of a house, one knows at once there is a wedding or other reception going on, or is going to take place.

At a wedding reception, the arrival of the guests is generally between 2 and 3.30 p.m. The number of guests at these receptions sometimes amounts to hundreds, but when this is the case it is usually given at a good hotel.

The arrangements for serving the refreshments on these occasions are similar to those explained for a stand-up luncheon in the previous chapter.

The guests on arriving at the place are shown into their corresponding cloak-rooms, and then to the reception-room, at the entrance of which they are met by the usher (appropriately dressed for the occasion) who, after reading their cards, announces their names in a more or less loud voice according to previous instructions received from the hostess. The host and hostess (the bride's parents) receive the guests at the entrance of the reception room, and the bride and bridegroom also shake hands with the guests as they enter and receive congratulations.

Of course, a grand display of choice flowers and large palms is *de rigueur* on these occasions, and is chiefly responsible for the big item for extras figuring on the bill a few days later.

# CHAPTER 17

# BALL SUPPERS

There is perhaps more variety in waiting at a ball-supper table than at any other meal.

In a private house, the number of guests invited to a ball-supper is never very great; consequently the arrangement of the tables is not a matter of great difficulty; for either one or two large tables, or several small ones, are arranged and laid out according to the shape and size of the dining-room.

The manner of laying these tables is almost the same as for a luncheon or dinner, except that large soup-spoons are not laid, and the number and size of the glasses to be used depends on the wines to be served.

A few extra flowers and smilax are generally used on these occasions to beautify the tables.

With the exception of the first three courses, namely the *consommé*, fish, and cutlets, which are hot, the rest of the dishes are cold and should be placed on the *buffet* or sideboard, provided that the room is not too warm, as otherwise they are sure to get spoiled.

The hot dishes are handed round one after the other in the usual way, but the cold ones are selected by the guests from the menu placed in front of them.

Ball suppers are greatly varied when given at a fashionable hotel or restaurant. Here, the arrangements and waiting required depend chiefly upon the price per head previously arranged by the host with the management; and as these suppers are given by a cosmopolitan public, their variety is unlimited.

Some patrons, from motives of economy or from complete lack of good taste, give most indifferent suppers; while others, on the other hand, by the brilliancy and refinement of these *fêtes*, make them the subject of comment in the Press. The Maître d'hôtel who superintends these suppers and the waiters under him must be men of great experience in the matter, if they are to successfully meet the requirements of the ever-exacting public.

Sit-down ball-suppers are served at these establishments between 12 and 2 a.m. either in the Restaurant, Table d'hôte Room, or in the Banqueting Hall, according to the number of guests and other circumstances.

The arrangement of tables may be either one long table down the length of the hall with smaller ones joined to it at intervals as used at big banquets, or a number of tables round and square placed about the room, each table seating any number from four to twenty.

When a large ball-supper is served at separate tables, it is always a source of worry and hard work for the waiters; for it often occurs that when all the tables are laid as per instructions previously received, and everything is ready and in order, some young gentlemen of the party will rush into the supper-room at the very last moment wanting to join up the tables of this and the other party, or making this and that arrangement, which, of course, necessitates shifting and changing of tables all over the room. This is rather annoying, as it disturbs the order and all arrangements previously made by the Maître d'hôtel for the proper seating of the guests.

At the majority of provincial hotels and the middle-class hotels in Town, the ball-supper is served by all the servants in the place; there is no off-duty for anybody on these occasions.

The linen-keeper and the head chamber-maid look after the ladies' cloak-room, and a couple of floor valets that of the gentlemen.

The carving of all large joints is done by the chef or one of his men behind the buffet.

The Head-waiter receives all orders concerning the supper, allocates the tables to the waiters, and gives them the necessary instructions to ensure a good and systematic service. At one o'clock, or at whatever hour it has been arranged for the supper to be served, he goes to the Ball-room and announces to the host and hostess that 'Supper is ready.' He immediately retires to the supper-room, where he receives and seats the guests, and directs operations throughout until the coffee is served.

The floor porters clear away the dirty plates, empty dishes, etc., the plate-men look after the silver and knives, the house-maids wipe plates and wash glasses during and after the supper. Every one is kept fully employed throughout the whole night and morning.

The manager, of course, supervises everywhere and studies the comfort and pleasure of the guests.

In addition to preparing the dining-room for supper, a large buffet must always be laid out in a convenient place, somewhere near the ball-room, to which the dancers resort at intervals for refreshments.

The following page shows a specimen menu for a sit-down ball-supper at a good establishment.

Stand-up *soirée* and ball-suppers are now almost a thing of the past; but when this is preferred, it consists of simple cold dishes and light refreshments only.

The chief arrangement for this is a large *ambigu*, or place where everything that is to be served is placed at once on a *buffet* or large table.

The corresponding plates, silver, glasses, etc., are also on the table or near at hand.

This kind of supper is served in exactly the same way as a stand-up luncheon described in a preceding chapter.

The gentlemen generally wait on their lady partners.

The small tables in the *ambigu* should be prettily arranged with flowers, sandwiches, French pastries, etc. Only small plates and dessert spoons and forks need be laid, as nothing requiring knives is served.

If special wine-butlers are not provided, the waiters who attend to the tables open the Champagne and pour out the Hock and Claret-cup as required.

Although the guests, especially the gentlemen, help themselves to the good things provided, waiters are occasionally required to hand round sandwiches, sweets, etc., and must be always on the alert to make themselves useful in this respect.

# SOUPER DE BAL

| | |
|---|---|
| *Consommé Riche en Tasse* | Rich Consommé in cups |
| — | — |
| *Filets de Soles Frits* | Fried Fillets of Soles |
| *Sauce Tatare* | and Tartar Sauce |
| — | — |
| *Darnes de Saumon en Belle-vue* | Cold Salmon |
| *Mayonnaise de Homard* | Lobster Mayonnaise |
| — | — |
| *Noisettes de Pré-Salé* | Lamb Noisettes |
| *aux Petits Pois* | and Green Peas |
| *Pommes Chatouillard* | Chatouillard Potatoes |
| — | — |
| *Pâté de Perdreaux Truffé* | Truffled Partridge Pie |
| *Mousse de Jambon* | Ham and Foie Gras Mousse |
| *Mousse de Foie Gras* | Cold Lamb and Fillet of Beef |
| *Filet de Bœuf et d'Agneau Froids* | York Ham |
| *Jambon d'York* | Ox Tongue |
| *Langue à l'Écarlate* | Chicken Galantine in Aspic |
| *Galantine de Volaille en Aspic* | Dressed Quails and Larks |
| *Cailles et Mauviettes* | Russian Salad |
| *en Belle-vue* | — |
| *Salade Russe* | Pears Melba |
| — | Chocolate Bavarois |
| *Poires Melba* | Coffee Eclairs |
| *Bavarois au Chocolat* | Charlotte with Whipped Cream |
| *Éclairs au Café* | Stewed Fruit |
| *Charlotte à la Chantilly* | Neapolitan Ice |
| *Compôte de Fruits assortis* | Wafers and Friandises |
| *Glace Napolitaine* | — |
| *Gaufrettes et Friandises* | Coffee and Liqueurs |
| — | |
| *Café et Liqueurs* | |

When the guests at a sit-down supper number eight or nine hundred, and the supper-room can accommodate only a quarter or so of that number at once, the guests must perforce be served at four or more different sittings. This means that immediately one party has finished, the waiters must clear away the things and relay the tables as quickly as possible. To facilitate the service on such an occasion each waiter should not wait on more than six guests. A good number of extra hands should also be on duty in the pantry, plate-room and the kitchen.

One of the most brilliant balls and suppers given in London is the famous Caledonian Ball given annually at the renowned Hotel Cecil in the Strand.

The number of guests at this ball is always well over 2,000.

Although this Hotel is the largest establishment of its kind in Europe and contains many spacious halls, it is not always possible to serve all the guests at one sitting.

# CHAPTER 18

# GARDEN-PARTIES

Garden-parties are of an informal nature, as guests of all ages spend the afternoon leisurely in the way that pleases them best. The 'sportive' section among them spend their time either in looking on or taking part in a game of lawn-tennis or croquet, while others stroll about or, standing or sitting, chat in groups until it is announced that 'Tea is served.'

At some Garden-parties tea is served to the guests standing. Large silver two-handled trays containing cups of tea and coffee are handed round by waiters, followed by others with several kinds of sandwiches, cut bread and butter, cut cake, assorted pastries, biscuits, etc.

Arrangements are generally made to suit any guests who prefer to take their tea seated at small tables.

When the refreshments are served in the dining-room, or in a tent in the garden, a long table is laid in the centre of the room or a *buffet* erected at the end of the tent containing, if the guests are numerous, two large urns with all the other items just mentioned, as well as lemonade and Hock or Claret-cup, in large glass jugs, and corresponding glasses, cups, sugar-basins and cream-jugs.

In proportion to the number of guests, it is well to put a number of small tea-tables in the garden and round the place where tea is served. These must, of course, be nicely laid out with everything ready to serve the guests. A small vase of flowers should be placed on each small table and two or three large ones on the large centre table and the buffet.

The tea and coffee are served in the usual way by the servants of the house, or by hired waiters.

As the cups, plates, sugar, milk, cream, etc., are placed on the small tables beforehand, when tea is ordered by a party it is only necessary to bring in, on a silver tray, a tea-pot, a jug of boiling water, pastries, and bread and butter.

As these gatherings always take place in the summer, various kinds of ices are also served as a matter of course. The ice-cream is served on small frosted-glass plates, and when serving this to a guest, the waiter should place on the table a plate of ice wafers.

It is also customary to serve strawberries and cream on these occasions, either before or after the tea. If plain strawberries and cream are served, a dessert plate and dessert spoon and fork must be laid for each guest, and a nicely dressed fruit dish or basket of strawberries is placed in the centre of the table. A jug of thick cream and a basin of castor sugar are placed beside the strawberries.

Finger-bowls should be put on the table with this service, as guests use their fingers to remove the stalks of the strawberries. If the strawberries are already prepared, *i.e.* with the cream poured over them, no finger-bowls are required.

93

Strawberries may be prepared for table in many different ways, each excellent in itself. One very good way which generally meets with the approval of epicures, is *à la Cecil*. To prepare a portion of strawberries *à la Cecil** sufficient for four or five guests, put in a silver timbale the strained juice of two large ripe oranges and one lemon; add three or four tablespoonfuls of castor sugar and stir. Neatly remove the stalks of the strawberries without bruising them and drop them in the juice. Stir gently so that they are well soaked, and leave them for five minutes in the ice box or in the freezer to macerate. Half fill a bowl with finely crushed ice and bury the timbale in the bowl (a special double timbale should be used for the purpose). Stir the strawberries gently once more, and add about half a pint of thick cream. Stir again and serve.

A prominent Lord, dining at the Cecil Restaurant with a well-known society lady, not very long ago, pronounced this preparation 'simply delicious', and the lady, 'a perfect *rêve*.'

---

* This is one of the many specialities served at the Hotel Cecil Restaurant, London.

94

# PICNICS AND
# AL-FRESCO LUNCHEONS

It is not often that people lunch in the open air; the only occasions being at the races, when hunting or getting up a picnic, or
similar pleasure parties.

When a repast of this kind is given by a lady or a gentleman,
the catering arrangements are generally entrusted to a well-
known catering firm who make a speciality of these affairs. In
this way the whole service gives satisfaction to the participants
of the function, without trouble to the givers of these parties,
and materially enhances their reputation as a successful host or
hostess.

These catering firms undertake to supply everything; from
the tents, tables and waiters, down to the tooth-picks, and do

everything to relieve clients as far as possible of the trouble of having to solve for themselves the problem of the 'luncheon hamper.'

At a Race meeting it is usual for the parties to lunch on the top or inside of the coach or car, or wherever most convenient. On these occasions the waiter or waiters who look after the provisions must be smart and never lose sight of the hampers; as there generally are many hungry folk about who cannot well afford Galantine truffée nor Pommery Extra Dry, and they cause these to frequently vanish.

For *Al-fresco* luncheons in the open country, these firms supply most convenient 'Luncheon table hampers', which are constructed in such an ingenious manner as to allow a most excellent and *recherché* luncheon with all the necessaries to be served in a few minutes.

The ready-dressed dishes are placed on the table with all the requisites for serving them.

The gentlemen, as a rule, help the ladies and themselves.

The waiters make themselves useful in removing the dirty plates, etc., opening the champagne and pouring it out, or setting the bottles on the table for the guests to help themselves.

Whether these repasts are served in the open field or in a country house, the man in charge of the hampers must be extremely careful not to forget any of the accessories of the meal. It often happens that on going to open the champagne it is found that the packer forgot to include a corkscrew and wire-nippers, or perhaps the glasses, the bread, the salt or the salad dressing.

These *contretemps* tend to mar the best appointed of repasts. To prevent this, a list should be made the previous day of all the provisions and everything necessary to make a really nice service, and then ticked off as they are placed in the hamper.

| MENU | MENU |
|---|---|
| FOR AN AL-FRESCO LUNCHEON | FOR A HUNT BREAKFAST |
| *Hors-d'œuvre Variés* | *Olives Espagnoles* |
| | *Salami* |
| *Mayonnaise de Saumon* | *Jambon Fumé* |
| *Médaillons de Homard* | *Artichauts Poivrades* |
| *à la Russe* | |
| | *Aspic de Homard* |
| *Bœuf braisé à la Gelée* | *à l'Américaine* |
| *Jambon d'York* | *Saumon à la Montpellier* |
| *Poulet Rôti. Langue* | |
| *à l'Écarlate* | *Terrine de Bœuf à la Mode* |
| *Galantine de Volaille* | *Poularde à la Neva* |
| *Pâte de Foie Gras Truffé* | *Jambon d'York à la Gelée* |
| *Suprêmes de Volaille St.-James* | *Hure de Sanglier aux Pistaches* |
| *Salade Cœurs de Laitues* | *Galantine de Perdreaux* |
| | *Bœuf Pressé. Langue de Bœuf* |
| *Gelée Macédoine* | *Salade Japonaise Collée* |
| *Crème Parisienne* | |
| *Gâteau Princesse* | *Macédoine aux Liqueurs* |
| *Blancmange aux Amandes* | *Mousse aux Fraises* |
| *Pâtisserie assortie* | *Petits Fours* |
| *Dessert* | *Dessert* |
| *Café* | *Café* |

The preceding menus are intended just as samples of what can be contained in a hamper of this kind.

# CHAPTER 20

# TABLE MANNERS AND FOODS OF THE NATIONS

However bad a reputation our English climate may have with most people, English table manners are reputed to be the best in all the world, and it is a thousand pities that certain other nations do not copy our behaviour at table, or establish schools in their own country for the study of table deportment.*

The progress of nations in refinement on matters appertaining to the table is best ascertained by a survey of the different kinds of food they relish and consume.

---

* Educated people of all nations, possessing refinement and good-breeding, are excluded from the following remarks.

Any one who has travelled leisurely through different countries and observed the *mœurs* of the inhabitants cannot have failed to be struck by the different kinds of food relished by the different nations, as well as their strange habits and behaviour at table.

Such a one, who has made these observations, can in a moment tell the nationality of a diner-out in a public restaurant by the dishes he chooses and the manner of manipulating his knife and fork.

Brillat-Savarin never penned a better truism than when he wrote, 'Say what you eat and I will tell you what you are'; and his aphorism stands good for the present generation.

Has anyone ever watched two Germans eating, seated opposite one another and discussing business?

If you have not, just ask anybody in the City who lunched before the war at restaurants frequented by German stockbrokers, near the Exchange, and listen to their impressions. They are sure to tell that by the way they flourished the knives and forks, anyone might think they were fighting a duel with swords!

One of them alone, when he is eating, makes more noise than twenty Englishmen together; and when a party of Germans is in a restaurant, the band cannot be heard while they are drinking their soup.

They like and eat 'Tartar Steak' consisting of raw meat and raw onions chopped. They consume huge quantities of 'Bismarck Pickled Herrings', *Schweinfleisch*, *Sauerkraut*, and German Sausages.

The average one amongst them when at table, if seen from a distance, might easily be thought to be conducting a band.

They talk coarsely to the waiter, eat with their knives, and are noted for being beer swillers.

The Austrians and Hungarians, though having much in common with the Germans, are of much finer type and style, and their table-manners are decidedly more refined. Viennese cookery is certainly nice.

The Russians are not yet quite up-to-date with matters concerning the table. Their Bortsch, their Caviare, and their *Charlotte Russe* are certainly excellent; but their *cuisine répertoire* is very limited. Their food consists chiefly of salt fish, smoked ham and salmon. They begin their meals with raw spirits such as Vodka, and finish with a cup of plain tea with a slice of lemon in it.

The Turks' chief food is rice cooked with very little meat cut up in small pieces. This is sometimes varied by salt fish. The Turks are on the whole temperate and eat great quantities of dry fruit, chiefly figs.

The Brazilian and the Portuguese people have much in common regarding their food. Their favourite dishes are *Bacalhao com batatas* (salt cod fish cooked with green oil, onions, garlic, tomatoes and potatoes); also boiled rice with chopped hard-boiled eggs, stewed meat with tomatoes and potatoes strongly flavoured with garlic, and their national dish *Feijoada* (baked black haricot beans served with *mandioca* flour).

They eat large quantities of tinned sardines and drink strong thick red wine for breakfast; tea or coffee is seldom taken at this repast. They are very partial to all sweet dishes and eat a good deal of jam with the spoon in the same way that people here eat porridge.

With regard to their manners at table, the less said about them the better.

The Argentine people partake of everything eatable, but have no real idea of what *cuisine* means. The population of the

Argentine Republic is composed of 50 per cent *creollos* (real natives), 25 per cent Italians, and 25 per cent German and English.

The best businesses such as the Railways, the Docks, the Electric Lighting, the Tramways and *Frigorificos*, by the way, are in the hands of the English.

The *creollos* love their native dish *Puchero*, which consists of beef, bacon, chicken, vegetables and rice, cooked together in a pot; also, *Asado con cuero* and *Bife à caballo* (a grilled steak with two fried eggs on top). They put their elbows on the table, pick their teeth freely, and carry a toothpick in their mouths long after a meal is finished.

Italians do not eat much meat, due perhaps to the hot climate in which they live, but are very fond of *Risotto*, *Menestrone*, *Polenta*, *Raviolis*, *Gnocchi*, and *Macaronis*.

They drink strong red wine (in moderation), are particularly partial to green oil and garlic in their cookery, and eat a great deal of ice-cream and sweets.

If they happen to be at table with intimate friends they are very talkative, and gesticulate energetically with their hands and whole body.

Spanish people eat hardly any meat or fish, but consume great quantities of cereals; rice, haricot beans, *garbanzos*, and peas. They also eat quantities of olives, green vegetables, salad and fruit, all of which abound in that sunny country.

Chocolate, which is made very thick, is as popular a beverage in Spain as tea is in England.

A Spanish breakfast generally consists of chocolate with *Bollos de leche*, or *Tostadas con manteca*. Their national dish is the *Puchero à la Castellana*, which is a complete dish in itself, being composed of beef, ham, chicken, and *chorizo*, cooked together with *garbanzos* and cabbages. They love *Paella à la Valenciana*, *Olla podrida*, and in summer-time *Gaspacho* (a special bread salad flavoured with pounded almonds and garlic). They do not drink a great deal of wine (although it is very cheap there), but water with *azucarillos* and *aguardiente* or syrup, which they call *refrescos*.

France is the country of the real *cuisine par excellence*; there almost everybody lives well and partakes of everything that is eatable, including *grenouilles et escargots* (frogs and snails).

French people are most particular about what they eat, and more especially the way in which it is cooked.

The *Pot-au-feu* is considered the dish of the working-class, and their *Petite Marmite* is the soup most frequently served at the best appointed tables everywhere.

Although extremely particular about their food, they are not so about their manners at table. They talk loudly, tuck their serviette in their shirt-collar, make a great display with the *cure-dent*, and sit with their elbows on the table.

As is well known, there is a large percentage of people in France who eat horseflesh in preference to beef.

The majority of the men drink *absinthe* before their meals, red or white wine during meals, and strong black coffee afterwards.

The United States of America embraces perhaps a greater variety of people than any other country in the world. China, Japan, Turkey and all the European nations are represented there—each with a large proportion of its people. The Asiatic people's food consists mainly of rice with very little meat or fish.

The average American partakes of almost anything (even of tortoises, which he calls 'Terrapins'), but is far from being an epicure. They like to have all the dishes placed in front of them, and then eat three or four different things at the same time. They are particularly fond of cereals for breakfast, such as Grape-nuts, Quaker-oats, corn-on-cob, hominy fritters, and buckwheat cakes with golden syrup.

Their national dishes are corned beef, planked shad, baked beans, and beef-hash; any one of them eats more salad than ten rabbits. They are noisy in the dining-room, disregard refinement, pick their teeth, spread their arms on the table, and talk boisterously.

When dining at a restaurant, they love to have a confidential chat and crack a joke with the Maître d'hôtel in charge.

They never omit to let you know they hail from America, in case you have failed to notice their nasal twang.

Of the United Kingdom, or England, as we like to call it, much could be said with regard to food and table habits.

Ireland and Scotland, which form part of this 'God's own country', have some very appetising national dishes. 'Irish stew' was not long ago pronounced by the patrons of a large catering firm in London (who had a sort of poll for dishes) to be the favourite dish, and insisted upon the management including it every day in the Bill of Fare as a permanent *Plat du Jour.*

Scotch people are proud of their 'haggis' and 'hotchpotch', and not in a small measure of their whisky.

There is a great deal of difference in the volubility of these two while at table. The Scotchman does not talk much while dinner is going on, and does not miss much from the menu; whilst the Irishman talks a great deal and gesticulates much as an Italian does.

Of the two, the Irishman is more refined and temperate at table.

The food grown or manufactured in England is the best in the world; and with the exception of wine and tropical fruit, there is nothing that cannot be grown here. The one great drawback is, however, that it is impossible for England to produce enough for its great population.

The number of bullocks, sheep, etc., consumed in England is enormous compared with that of other nations, and it is a good thing for us that such good supplies are always forthcoming from Australia and the Argentine Republic.

The average Englishman does not care much for soup; his food is substantial and his table generally well provided with good things.

If he does not partake of a large joint, a pie or pudding, and Cheddar or Stilton cheese, accompanied by a good supply of wine or beer, he does not think he has made a good dinner.

CHAPTER 21

# REMARKABLE TABLES AND FREAK DINNERS GIVEN BY WEALTHY PEOPLE

Were I to attempt to describe all the extraordinary dinners, or rather freak feasts given by eccentric people, both in England and America, during the last few years, I could certainly write many pages on the subject.

The managers of the modern large hotels, both in London and America, assisted by their army of well-trained staff, have from time to time astonished the world by their ingenuity in getting up all kinds of remarkable banquets.

In fact, the modern *Hôtelier*'s enterprise seems to have no limit in this direction.

Should a wealthy patron desire to entertain his friends to a dinner at the North or South Pole, on an aeroplane, in a farmyard, or at the bottom of the sea, the modern *Hôtelier* or *Restaurateur* will, as if by magic, transform a large banqueting hall into a wonderful resemblance of either of these places; a resemblance so wonderfully effective as to make you marvel, and in fact almost make you think it was the real place.

Not long ago, one of these remarkable dinners was given in London by the late Mr. Alfred G. Vanderbilt, the well-known American millionaire, to celebrate the winning of a Horse Show prize at Olympia with his famous team of horses.

The table was shaped as a picture-frame; six covers were laid at the top of the table, six at the bottom, and twelve at either side. In the centre, at a lower elevation, was a representation of a coach meet; real turf, roads, small trees, etc., being used. The whole idea was wonderfully effective and the Press was very eulogistic as to the excellence of the arrangements and the appropriate good taste of the scheme of decoration used.

Some of the dinners given by wealthy Americans while sojourning in London are splendid, and the ingenious arrangements and effect of their tables remarkable indeed.

A notable one was given at the Savoy Hotel by Mr. G.A. Kessler, to some partisans of Peary and Cook, the American explorers.

The room, a large one, was transformed to represent the North Pole. The dinner-table stood in the middle and was round in the shape of a large well; its centre was full of artificial snow, where the figures of Peary and Cook could be seen trying to reach the summit. Thirty-two guests sat round in white chairs; whilst the waiters and other attendants were dressed in Polar-bear skins and looked like real Esquimaux.

Of the several famous places for novelty in banquets in New York, Delmonico Restaurant and Knickerbocker's Hotel are perhaps the most popular of all in America.

At these places, the wealthy eccentrics may be seen any day dining on horseback, dressed as cow-boys, or sitting on stools and using empty champagne cases as tables, seeming to return to the simple life for a dinner, in distinctly primitive manner.

One of the dinner-party giving crazes that prevailed for some time in America was termed 'Dinner and Dance in a Farm-yard.'

The invitation cards ran thus:

> Farmer and Mrs. —— will be pleased if you 'kan kom' on the ——,
> at ........... o'clock, to their farmhouse (here address).
> There will be a dance in the barn. They also will be glad if you would
> like to have a 'bite' with them in the farmyard; if so, please bring your
> own fork and knife, as there may be a shortage of these implements.
> You need not dress much to 'kom.' If you haven't no new Sunday
> clothes, please 'kom' as you are; for it ain't going to be no eticket,
> as our freends don't like no fuss.

These rustic dinner-parties were held both at private houses and at hotels and restaurants; either several large rooms or the whole basement used to be transformed into a veritable farmhouse, and the dancing place converted into a genuine barn. Everything was real with regard to livestock and implements. The walls were adorned here and there with hay-rakes, pitchforks, scythes, bundles of hay, corn-cribs, harness, etc., and almost all the inhabitants of Noah's Ark were represented there alive, and allowed to run or to fly about amongst the guests.

The host and hostess were dressed up in real farmer's clothes on these occasions.

The dinner-table decoration was also appropriate for the occasion. Real turf covered the table centre; and miniature cattle-troughs full of water, hay-stacks, barns and farmhouses, as well as pigs, ducks, geese, chicken, pigeons, rabbits, cows and horses grazing, were the chief ornaments.

———

One rather picturesque dinner served at one of these hotels was given by the president of a Golf Club to some of his intimate friends. The table was arranged as a golf course, with miniature trees, bunkers, a lake and a green.

———

The greatest eccentricity so far as dinners go, I consider are 'Jungle Picnics.' In America these seem to be one of the latest crazes, and there are few people of the smart set who cannot boast of having lunched in a lions' den.

At one of these feasts an amateur lion tamer gave his friends an entertainment with four full-grown lions from Bostock's Menagerie.

During the dinner the animals roamed about the room at will, and were treated with the same dainty dishes as the guests.

As was to be expected, there were many exciting incidents; although the majority of the guests were daring in the extreme, it was amusing to see some of them suddenly turn pale and jump to their feet when discovering a monarch of the forest snuffling at their elbows.

A very wealthy lady of Chicago, noted for her daring feats as an expert climber in Switzerland, once gave a dinner on the roof of her house. The guests, being all amateur climbers, were previously invited to attend the dinner in mountaineer garb. The house was transformed into a miniature copy of Mont Blanc; the lady herself received the guests at the entrance, and after being fastened with ropes in the usual manner, they climbed to the summit guided by the hostess, where a sumptuous dinner was waiting for the merry mountaineers.

———

Never was there such a topsy-turvy affair as the 'Upside-down' dinner given on January 16th, 1914, by Hendon airmen at the Royal Automobile Club, in London, to Mr. B.C. Hucks and Mr. Gustave Hamel in honour of their 'looping the loop' and 'upside-down' flying.

The usual order of dinner was reversed, and the meal ended with the *Hors-d'œuvre*, the menu being as follows:

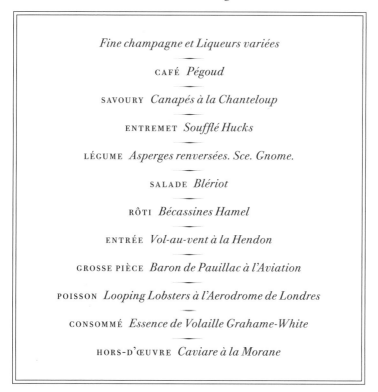

*Fine champagne et Liqueurs variées*

———

CAFÉ  *Pégoud*

———

SAVOURY  *Canapés à la Chanteloup*

———

ENTREMET  *Soufflé Hucks*

———

LÉGUME  *Asperges renversées. Sce. Gnome.*

———

SALADE  *Blériot*

———

RÔTI  *Bécassines Hamel*

———

ENTRÉE  *Vol-au-vent à la Hendon*

———

GROSSE PIÈCE  *Baron de Pauillac à l'Aviation*

———

POISSON  *Looping Lobsters à l'Aerodrome de Londres*

———

CONSOMMÉ  *Essence de Volaille Grahame-White*

———

HORS-D'ŒUVRE  *Caviare à la Morane*

Everything was upside-down. The two guests of honour sat under large mirrors which reflected them 'upside-down' at a table which was weirdly arranged in the form of a loop. The table legs pointing upwards helped the idea.

The most remarkable feature of this original dinner was that at the end of it nearly all confessed that they felt hungry. Some even suggested the plan of following the 'upside-down' dinner with one 'right-side-up.'

When dinner was over many of the guests tried to describe their feeling on the back of their menu card. A guest of honour wrote: 'The dinner requires even more practice to enjoy, than flying.'

When Mr. Hucks responded to the toast of his health he began with 'Lastly' and went on 'Thirdly', and finished up with a sentence which began 'Firstly.'

---

The Grafton Galleries have witnessed many a brilliant gastronomic affair. The *Souper Artistique* at which Mr. Jan Van Beers (the South Africa magnate) entertained a large party of his London friends was certainly a unique entertainment, and deserves record. The menu was an excellent one. The decorations were remarkably tasteful, but the *souper* will be principally remembered for the series of surprises with which it was accompanied. Thus: the electric light was suddenly switched off, whereupon the table and guests became mysteriously illuminated from an unseen source. It was then evident that the table was a sheet of glass under the cloth, and that the lights were beneath it.

Two *Pâtés* were handed to the host, who promptly released from them some dozens of tame Java Sparrows, who hopped and twittered about the room.

The temporary ceiling was a *velarium*, and hereupon was thrown, by a magic lantern, figures from *Vanity Fair* of several of the guests and others. Madame Melba 'came on' from the opera to sing; Miss Florence St. John also sang. Both were accompanied by Mr. Ganz in a Court suit. This famous *Souper Artistique* was mentioned in all the leading Society papers.

———

Of the many freak dinner-parties lately given in America there has not perhaps been one that has caused so much merriment amongst its guests as that given by Mr. and Mrs William Schall of Chicago, called 'The Baby Dinner-Party.'

The guests were the most distinguished people in American capital. Both ladies and gentlemen were dressed as babies, and carried feeding-bottles round their necks; the bottles were filled with the beverage selected by each baby guest. Every one of them carried also a collection of toys, rattles and squeaking dolls. Throughout the dinner, yells and baby cries were frequently imitated, which created much amusement amongst the guests.

The dinner was followed by a dance which lasted till the early hours of the next morning.

———

The present Marconi House in the Strand has been the scene of the most-talked-of dinner in London when that place was known as 'The New Gaiety Restaurant.' Some years ago, a group of very wealthy gentlemen, who had made their piles in the South African mines, conceived the idea of giving a characteristic dinner of their earlier days to their friend and colleague Mr. Harry Barnato.

For this purpose they engaged several adjoining rooms at the 'New Gaiety Restaurant' and had them transformed into a veritable South African mining camp. Of course, the pictures, fine furniture, carpets, etc., were removed beforehand. In a large saloon they erected a tent, and at the entrance of it they cooked (or rather pretended to) the dinner in a huge caldron.

The diners themselves were dressed up for the occasion in the old Boer fashion, and there were special men dressed up as Boers and Kaffirs posted at the entrance to greet the party on entering the camp.

The dinner-table was laid inside the tent in a very primitive manner. From the ceiling there hung a few old-fashioned lanterns; the place of candelabras was taken by tallow-candles stuck in empty bottles, and wooden stools instead of chairs.

The dinner and the wines were supplied by the restaurant and were of the very best. The dishes on the menu bore strange denominations which, no doubt, had great significance to the diners on that occasion.

---

The words *'Gentlemen!'* 'We will now lunch on the face of time, for the first time', were printed in bold type on the front page of the 'Menu-Souvenir' of a luncheon held at the 'Trades Hall' in Leicester, on November 18th, 1910, served on one of the four twenty-five feet (in diameter) dials of the world's biggest electric clock, manufactured by Messrs. Gent & Co., Ltd., at Faraday works, Leicester, for the offices of the Royal Liver Insurance Company at Liverpool.

This huge and wonderful clock is two feet larger than Big Ben, which since then has not got the proud position of being the biggest clock in the world.

Thirty-eight guests, including many commercial and railway notabilities, lunched round this unique 'Time-Table'.

The following is a copy of the (chronologically arranged) menu.

## MENU

Mock Turtle Soup
(*Served in face-plates*)

———

Mutton Cutlets
(*Bread-crumb insulation*)

———

Galantine of Tur(n)key
(*À la Ding-Dong*)

———

Pressed Beef
(*Use both hands*)

———

York Ham
(*From the 'big-end'*)

———

Salad
(*Without clock-oil*)

———

Raspberry Trifle
(*A trifle larger than Big Ben*)

———

Apple-tart
(*Cores removed, Hands off*)

———

Mince Pies
(*Currents alternating*)

———

Cheese and Celery
(*À la counterweight, from the cast-iron bed*)

———

'The man who broke the bank at Monte Carlo', as the newspapers called him at the time, was the host of a remarkable feast given some time ago at the Savoy Restaurant, Strand.

*L'amphitryon* of this special dinner-party had won a large amount of money on the *roulette* at Monte Carlo, and *Rouge* had been the colour responsible for his good fortune.

To celebrate his lucky event in an appropriate manner he invited thirty-six of his intimate friends to a dinner, which was the talk of everybody, and commented upon in the Press.

This feast was called amongst the people in the Hotel *Le Dîner Rouge et Noir*, but the Press referred to it as 'The Red Dinner at the Savoy', for everything from the ceiling to the carpet in the saloon was red. Even the waiters wore red costumes; and their shirts, ties and gloves were also red.

A magnificent display of beautiful and expensive flowers, and the electric lights, were of the same tint. And the dinner, as much as it was possible, together with the wines, which were of an elaborate and costly character, were of the same colour.

The menu was composed of *Prawns*, *Queues de Langouste en Aspic*, *Crème Portugaise*, *Saumon à la Nantua*, *Mousse au Jambon*, *Filet de Bœuf aux Tomates Farcies*, *Choux-Rouges braisés*, *Poularde à la Cardinal*, *Canard Sauvage au Sang*, *Salade de Betterave*, *Mousse aux Fraises*, etc.

The table itself represented a huge roulette, built especially to accommodate the same number of guests as there are numbers on the real roulette. In the centre of it there was a suggestive decoration made of beautiful flowers. The covers were numbered in the same order as on a real roulette, and were separated by red and black silk ribbons parting from the centre of the table. The number on which the money was won was to be seen everywhere in various shapes and ways in the room, and at this same number the host sat at the table.

The saloon and the table presented a wonderful spectacle, and the cost of the feast, it was rumoured, reached over four figures.

———

The Savoy Hotel in London has certainly been chosen by the wealthy eccentrics for their freak dinner-parties more frequently than any other Hotel in Europe.

It was at this same establishment that the famous 'Gondola Dinner' was given by Mr. George A. Kessler.

With just a little more than twenty four hours' notice, the manager and his staff accomplished a veritable *tour de force* of ingenuity and good taste on that occasion.

The host expressed to the manager his desire of giving a sumptuous dinner to some of his distinguished friends, and wanted it to be something quite out of the ordinary and a thing to be talked about.

After considering several schemes and suggestions from the manager, it was decided that the dinner should be served in a floating Venetian gondola.

The scene chosen for the dinner was the courtyard at the back of the building. This was made water-tight and filled with water several feet deep.

Many scores of hands were busy throughout the night and the next day, transforming the old courtyard into a miniature panorama of Venice.

They included engineers, carpenters, plumbers, upholsterers, electricians, and scene-painters. A score or more of tailors were also busy making costumes for the waiters, who were dressed as Venetian gondoliers.

The dinner-table was most artistically laid out inside the gondola; and this covered over with a canopy of white silk gauze.

Several little gondola boats and a number of swans could be seen gliding on the water; and the Italian airs played by the troupe of Venetian mandolinists during the dinner were delightful.

Both the table and the gondola, as well as the surroundings and the suite of rooms for the reception of the party, were most magnificently decorated with carnations and white roses; whilst the effects of the coloured electric lights were suggestive of Fairyland.

# CHAPTER 22

# THE ART OF CARVING

Carving has been looked upon as an art, and cultivated as such, ever since the days when the master of the house himself helped his friends and guests who were seated at his table to all the good things placed thereon for their entertainment; consequently, carving has since those early days been considered as an honourable and distinguished accomplishment.

At the present day, however, carving is held in high repute only among butlers and professional caterers, to whom this honour has been transferred since the establishment of the *service à la Russe*. No waiter, butler, Maître d'hôtel, or even a hotel or restaurant

Manager, is considered to be thoroughly competent unless he knows how to carve a joint and bird with dexterity. Carving ought to form part of the education of everybody, as it is such a useful accomplishment. If any one is suddenly called upon to carve on any particular occasion, it is always gratifying to that person to think that in doing so, he has been able to contribute largely to the success of the dinner and enjoyment of the guests, besides being able to show his adroitness and skill in the art.

The art of carving does not consist merely in cutting thin or thick slices from the joints served at table, but in cutting them economically and correctly according to their nature, and in distributing the portions quickly and skilfully.

The person appointed to carve the joint, or a large fish or bird at a dinner, must have and make use of his epicurean knowledge and not cause the dishes to lose anything of their appetising appearance.

To become a really good carver it is advisable to first of all watch some one who is an expert in the art, and afterwards practise by oneself for some time; for it is only by continual practice that one can become perfect.

All carving-knives should be well sharpened before the commencement of the dinner; for nothing irritates a good carver more than a blunt knife, and it is certainly far from pleasant to the guests to see or hear knives being sharpened while the dinner is getting cold.

In private houses, where a butler is not kept, the honour of carving the joint at table still devolves upon the master of the house; but in large establishments the butler is responsible for the carving. In hotels and restaurants, small things such as soles, pigeons, a porterhouse-steak, or a chicken, are carved by the waiter who is waiting on the party. But where there is a special party or parties with large joints and birds to be carved, the task of carving them devolves upon the Maître d'hôtel (in establishments where there is not a special carver), and he serves each guest with a portion and its accompanying sauce or gravy; or the cut slices are rearranged on the dish and then passed round, leaving the guests at liberty to help themselves.

Each dish should be sent to the table properly garnished, and the carver should preserve its arrangement as much as possible.

## FISH

In carving the turbot one should commence with the under-side (this side is always uppermost on the dish). This part is more esteemed than the back, which has a dark skin.

Make an incision and draw the knife down the middle of the body from the head to the tail; then other incisions at right angles from the central line, one-and-a-half inches apart. Each portion should be served with a little of the thick part and the gelatinous part of the fins. When the first side has been served, remove the bone and proceed in the same manner with the other side, taking care to remove the black skin.

*Note.*—In dealing with a large fish, such as cod, salmon, turbot, sturgeon, etc., it is very desirable that silver slices or silver-plated knives only should be used; as steel knives impart a very bad taste to fish.

In the case of salmon, first remove the skin from the upper side of the fish, as shown in the illustration; draw the knife down the middle of the back from the head to the tail, and divide into cross slices about an inch thick.

A large fried sole should be divided into two by making an incision from the head to the tail, and separate the two halves with the knife and fork; remove the bone before serving. A boiled sole is better carved with a tablespoon and fork. Pass the spoon round the sole so as to separate the fins from the fillets; make an incision from head to tail and remove the fillets neatly. Two fillets of a medium-sized sole form a proper portion for one person; the two fillets being neatly placed on the plate and a spoonful of sauce poured over them.

## MEAT

Beef and ham should always be carved very thinly.

The method of carving a ham varies. When carved by a professional, for profit, it is cut in very thin slices beginning at the knuckle end, towards the thick part of the ham. In a private establishment the butler carves the ham less economically in cross-slices, from the '*noix*', or what is popularly known as the 'Pope's Eye', under which is the choicest and most finely grained meat. When the ham is boned and rolled, the slices are cut vertically from top to bottom across the fibres in the same way as a galantine. To carve ham with ease, it should be placed on a special pedestal or ham-stand on which it rests securely. The carving knives must be long and flexible and well sharpened; otherwise it is almost impossible to carve satisfactorily.

If the slices of ham are served hot on plates, the gravy or sauce (if any) and accompanying vegetables should be served separately.

Saddle of mutton or lamb may be carved either lengthwise or transversely. Make a cut with the knife down the middle of the back from end to end; then divide into slices.

The slices should have a little fat adhering to them and be served with a spoonful of the gravy surrounding the joint.

To carve a leg of mutton or lamb, it is necessary to ascertain the position of the 'Pope's Eye'; for, as with the ham, this is the part most preferred. The joint should be dished up with this side uppermost and cut in slices as shown.

## POULTRY

In dealing with a capon or fat pullet, pass the knife round the legs, remove and divide into two by the joints, and place them on one end of the silver dish; then cut the wings, leaving a little of the breast adhering, and take one or two undercuts from each side. Now separate the remainder of the breast from the carcass and cut it in two. These ten or twelve pieces must then be rearranged on the dish (if the latter is to be passed round). In carving a fowl great care must be taken that the slices do not come into contact with either the gravy or the carving-board or dish, in order that the whiteness and fine appearance of the clean cuts are preserved.

A goose is one of the largest birds to carve, and is usually served up stuffed and roasted. It is placed with the breast towards the carver. The legs are detached without quite removing them, and portions from both sides of the breast are cut in thin slices. A little gravy is served on each plate together with half a spoonful of the stuffing.

To carve a Rouen duck or a wild duck, first detach the two legs and the two wings, and place them on the carving board. This done, it suffices to hold the wings firmly with the fork to enable the carver, after removing the skin, to cut off thin slices.

Young partridges, grouse and pigeons are simply split open with the knife along the middle; if large, make three portions.

The Guinea-fowl is carved as a chicken, *viz.*, the legs are cut in two, then the wings are detached, and the rest of the breast cut away from the carcass.

The breast of a roast pheasant should be carved in rather thin slices and replaced on the dish to be handed round, followed by the gravy, bread sauce, and bread-crumbs.

The turkey is carved as follows: Pass the knife round the legs and detach them without quite removing them. Detach first one and then the other wing, leaving a little meat adhering, to be served to those guests who have a preference for these brown parts. Next, cut thin slices from the breast as when carving a ham. Do not forget that gravy and cranberry sauce usually accompany the turkey.

# CHAPTER 23

# WHEN FOOD IS IN SEASON

Owing to the modern facilities and the swiftness with which food is imported in perfect condition from all parts of the globe into our markets, there are but few foods which cannot be obtained in England all the year round.

The believers in the proverb 'There is a season for everything, and everything should be eaten in season', will, I hope, find the following alphabetical list of edibles useful, as it shows when they are most plentiful and in their prime condition in England.

| | |
|---|---|
| Almonds (green) | *from May to July* |
| Anchovies | *all the year round* |
| Apples (various kinds) | *all the year round* |
| Apricots | *from May to August* |
| Artichokes (green) | *from December to June* |
| (Jerusalem) | *from October to February* |
| Asparagus (Argenteuil) | *from June to August* |
| (English) | *from July to September* |
| (forced, English and French) | *from January to end of May* |
| Bananas | *all the year round* |
| Barbel | *from July to March* |
| Bass | *from May to September* |
| Bigarroons | *from May to July* |
| Blackcock (shooting) | *from August 20 to December 12* |
| Brill | *from August to March* |
| Broad Beans | *from June to August* |
| Broccoli | *from October to end of April* |
| Brussels Sprouts | *from October to March* |
| Capsicums (tinned) | *all the year round* |
| Cardoons | *from November to May* |
| Carp | *from August to February* |
| Carrots (new) | *from May to June* |
| Cauliflowers | *from March to November* |
| Celeriac | *from October to March* |
| Celery | *from August to March* |
| Cherries | *from May to August* |
| Chestnuts | *from November to February* |
| Chic-Chickens (poussins) | *from April to May* |
| (spring) | *from April to June* |
| Cob Nuts | *from August to December* |
| Cod Fish | *all the year round* |
| Cod's Roe | *from February to April* |
| Corn-on-Cob (American) | *from August to October* |

| | |
|---|---|
| Cranberries | *from November to February* |
| Crawfish (Langouste) | *from June to September* |
| Crayfish (Écrevisse) | *from July to February* |
| Cucumbers | *from April to August* |
| Currants (all kinds) | *from May to September* |
| Damsons | *from August to October* |
| Ducks | *all the year round* |
| Eels | *from September to May* |
| Endive (French) | *from November to March* |
| (Belgian) | *from November to March* |
| Figs (fresh) | *from August to October* |
| Filberts | *from August to November* |
| Flageolets | *from July to September* |
| Flounders | *from August to April* |
| French Beans | *from June to October* |
| Geese | *from September to February* |
| Gooseberries | *from April to July* |
| Grapes (of various kinds) | *all the year round* |
| Greengages | *from June to September* |
| Grouse (shooting) | *from August 12 to December 12* |
| Halibut | *all the year round* |
| Hares (shooting) | *from August 1 to end of February* |
| Herrings | *from August to February* |
| Indian corn-on-cob | *from August to November* |
| Lamb (grass) | *from February to August* |
| Larks | *from September to March* |
| Lettuces (English) | *from May to September* |
| (French) | *from October to March* |
| Lobsters | *from June to September* |
| Mackerel | *from April to October* |
| Maize (American Corn-on-Cob) | *from August to October* |
| Medlars | *from November to January* |
| Melons (English) | *from May to September* |

| | |
|---|---|
| (Cantaloup) | *from July to October* |
| (Spanish) | *from July to February* |
| (Water) | *from July to February* |
| Mulberries | *from August to September* |
| Mullets | *from April to November* |
| Mushrooms (fresh) | *from March to October* |
| (forced, French and English) | *all the year round* |
| Mussels | *from September to April* |
| Nectarines | *from July to October* |
| Oranges (various kinds) | *all the year round* |
| Ortolans | *from May to September* |
| Oysters | *from September 1 to end of April* |
| Parsnips | *from October to April* |
| Partridges (shooting) | *from September 1 to end of January* |
| Peaches (hot-house and other) | *from May to October* |
| Pears | *from August to December* |
| Peas (green) | *from July to October* |
| Perch | *from July to March* |
| Pheasants (shooting) | *from October 1 to end of January* |
| Pigeons (Bordeaux) | *from August to March* |
| Pine-apples | *all the year round* |
| Plaice | *from May to January* |
| Plovers | *from October to March* |
| Plovers' eggs | *from April to May* |
| Plums | *from July to October* |
| Pomegranates | *from October to January* |
| Pork | *from October to April* |
| Prawns | *from May to October* |
| Ptarmigans | *from December to May* |
| Pumpkins | *from September to December* |
| Quails (from all parts) | *all the year round* |
| Quinces | *from October to February* |
| Raspberries | *from June to September* |

Rhubarb (forced and natural)    *from December to end of June*
Salmon (English)    *from March 1 to September 7*
  (Scotch)    *from February 11 to end of August*
Salsifis    *from October to March*
Scollops    *from September to end of April*
Seakale    *from December to May*
Shrimps    *from April to September*
Skate    *from September to end of April*
Snipes (shooting)    *from October 1 to March 15*
Soles    *from July to March*
Sorrel    *from April to August*
Spinach    *all the year round*
Sprats (fishing)    *from November 9 to end of March*
Strawberries (forced and other)    *from April to September*
Sturgeon    *from August to March*
Tangerines    *from November to June*
Teal Duck    *from October to end of February*
Tench    *from July to February*
Tomatoes    *all the year round*
Trout (river) (fishing)    *from April 1 to end of September*
  (Salmon) (fishing)    *from March 1 to September 7*
Truffles (fresh)    *from October to January*
Turbot    *all the year round*
Turkey    *from October to February*
Vegetable marrow    *from August to October*
Venison    *from July to end of February*
Walnuts (new)    *from September to December*
Watermelon    *from July to February*
Whitebait    *from February to September*
Whiting    *from August to February*
Widgeon    *from August to March*
Wild duck (shooting)    *from September to March*
Woodcocks (shooting)    *from October 1 to March 15*

# CHAPTER 24

# BOTTLING, THE CARE
# OF WINES AND THE CELLAR

An ideal wine-cellar is one which is built in such a way, and in such a place, as to effectively protect the bottles and the wine from being shaken or disturbed by vibration of heavy street traffic, or underground trains; also from frequent or sudden changes of temperature.

A uniform temperature is essential to the wine-cellar; and, in order to secure this as far as possible, the cellar should be fitted with double doors such as those used for refrigerators. On entering, care should be taken that the outer door is closed before opening the inner one.

The wine-cellar should have a concrete floor, as this is the most adequate for maintaining evenness of temperature. Sudden changes of temperature produce sourness in the wine, and in any case are most injurious.

One of the most important accessories to a well-appointed cellar is a good thermometer; and one of the chief duties of the butler or cellar-man is to keep the temperature day and night as near as possible to 50° Fahrenheit.

Good ventilation is also an essential to a well-appointed cellar. Hot or foul air is most detrimental to both beer and wine, especially if these are in casks.

Nothing but wine, beer and liqueurs should be kept in the cellar.

The most appropriate method of lighting the cellar is by electricity. All wine bottles must lie flat, so that the wine touches the corks. This prevents them from becoming dry, and the air in consequence turning the wine bad.

When bottling wine in the cellar, after making sure that the wine is matured and in proper condition to be bottled, the casks should be allowed to lie on a skid with the bung-hole uppermost for about a week or more before drawing, so as to allow the wine to become clear. The faucet must be introduced tightly into the cask before placing it on the skid. When the bottles to be filled have been thoroughly washed, they should be left to stand upside down for several days until they are perfectly dry. The corks must be quite new. To render them soft for use they should be soaked in hot water for about a quarter of an hour and then steeped in wine drawn from the cask.

The whole cask should be bottled off in one day, otherwise the wine remaining is sure to be affected and become unfit for bottling.

The bottles should not be filled to the top; an inch space should be left between the wine and the cork.

Before the bottles are binned, the necks should be steeped in melted wax to prevent the access of air to the wine through defective corks.

Bottles are often binned by inexperienced butlers without due regard to the temperature most suitable to each particular brand of wine.

In the coolest part of the cellar, Champagne and all sparkling wines such as Hock, Moselle or Burgundy should be placed.

All still (white) wines are better binned on the first three rows from the ground, these being the coolest, and all (red) Burgundy and Claret on the top bins, which are the warmest in the cellar.

This arrangement is, of course, for a cellar without partitions. In separated cellars the coolest one contains all sparkling and still-white wines, as well as the barrels of beer at a temperature of 50° Fahrenheit, and the other containing the red Burgundy, Claret, and Madeira, at 65° Fahrenheit as a medium temperature.

Should there be a difficulty in winter in maintaining 65° in this cellar, a hot steam-pipe round it, or one or two gas jets, will give the desired addition of temperature.

The rows of bins and the bins themselves should be numbered; and the name of the wine and its vintage also indicated.

The cellar must, of course, always be kept in darkness.

# CHAPTER 25

# THE CORRECT TEMPERATURE AND ORDER IN WHICH WINES SHOULD BE SERVED AT TABLE

In view of the diversity of tastes and opinions existing among the gourmets of different countries with respect to the wines that should be drunk with the different courses, it is rather a difficult problem to give an exact rule in fixing the number and nature of the wines, or the order in which they should be served at table.

At some private houses, when giving a little dinner-party, two or perhaps three kinds of wine only are served, *viz.*, Sherry and Claret or Burgundy, and Champagne.

When giving a banquet or a dinner at a restaurant, the task of ordering the wine lies with the giver of the feast. He selects from the wine-list the various kinds he wishes to offer his guests. When these have been definitely chosen by the host, the wine-butler orders them at the wine bar or cellar and it is his duty (in some places the Maître d'hôtel or the Head Waiter) to see not only that they are served just in time with the dishes for which they have been selected, but also to make sure, before pouring them out in the glasses, that they are at the temperature proper to each. All white wines, either Hock or Moselle, and Claret or Burgundies, must be served cold. In summer time the bottles are sent into the room in silver wine-coolers filled with ice. Champagne, except in winter, should always be served *frappé*.

With red wines it is just the reverse. In order to develop their characteristic *bouquet* they must be at the same temperature as the dining-room (said *Chambrés*), or just a little warmer. If at the moment of serving them they are at all cold, it is as well to take the chill off by placing the bottles in warm water for a few minutes.

Fine red wines, either Clarets or Burgundies, if they are old, contain sediment. On this account, before opening the bottles it is well to place them gently in a bottle-basket to perform the operation; and when pouring out the wine it must be done with extreme caution, so as not to shake the bottles.

When these fine wines are to be served at a special dinner it is always better to decant them in the cellar; as the possibility of disturbing the wine on the way to the table is thus avoided.

With regard to the wine drunk at table by people of different nations, the Americans' favourite drink at restaurants is Iced-water. The average English host or diner-out, either at a banquet or restaurant, takes a glass of Sherry with the soup, drinks Champagne extra dry throughout the dinner, and on special occasions finishes the dessert with a glass of old Port-wine or Claret.[*]

---

[*] Claret drinking after or with the dessert is a very old custom in England. Fortunately the modern epicure recognises this to be the wrong time for drinking Claret and the custom is fast disappearing.

This, of course, is purely a question of national custom and a matter of individual taste.

The object of this chapter is to show the various wines and the order of serving them with each course at a *recherché* dinner or a sumptuous banquet, according to the established custom of the best houses, both in England and on the Continent.

For instance: before the

### HORS-D'ŒUVRE

French or Italian Vermouth, Sherry and Angostura, Gin and Orange Bitters, Quinine Dubonett, Byrrh or an American cocktail. If among the guests at a large dinner-party there are Russian gentlemen, 'Vodka' is very welcome.

With the

### OYSTERS

Light white wines: either Burgundy or Claret, such as Chablis Moutonne or Montrachet, Château Carbonnieux, Sauterne or Haut Barsae.

Immediately after the

### SOUP

Dry Sherry: either Vino de Pasto, Oloroso or Jerez Amontillado.

With the

### REAL TURTLE SOUP

Madeira Wine or Milk Punch.

With

Still Hock, or those wines indicated for the Oysters.

With the

Entrées

Red Burgundy: either Beaujolais, Pommard, Nuits, Beaune, Volnay, Clos de Vougeot, Chambertin or Moulin-à-Vent.

With the

Relevé or joint

Red Claret: either Saint-Julien, Pontet Canet, Château Margaux, Château Laffitte, Ranzan Ségla or Léoville Lascasses.

With the

Roast and entremets

Champagne well iced.

With the

Dessert

Either Port-Wine, Vino Arropado, Gold-Malvasier, or Fine Muscats.

With the

Coffee

Old Fine Champagne, and either Kümmel, Bénédictine, or green or yellow Chartreuse, etc.

## A TABLE OF APPROXIMATE TEMPERATURES
## AT WHICH WINES SHOULD BE SERVED

| | |
|---|---|
| Sherry | 45° F |
| Madeira | 65° |
| White Burgundy | 45° |
| White Claret | 55° |
| Sparkling Hock and Moselle | 45° |
| Still Hock and Moselle | 55° |
| Red Burgundy | 70° |
| Red Claret | 65° |
| Champagne | 40° |
| Port Wine | 55° |
| Lager Beer | 40° |

# CHAPTER 26

# THE UNCORKING, DECANTING AND SERVING OF WINES

When a real connoisseur orders a costly bottle of fine wine from a French *sommelier* at a first-class French restaurant, he simply points to its number on the wine-list and does not trouble to make any observation as to the way in which the wine should be served; for he knows very well that the man with the chain round his neck thoroughly understands his business of handling and serving of wines.

If the wine admits of being well served without being decanted, he is sure to serve it without decanting it, as he knows well that a real connoisseur appreciates his wine much better in its original dusty or cobwebby bottle as it comes from the cellar, than in a stately decanter. Wine does not improve by being poured out of its own bottle into another vessel; not even though it be a costly jewelled decanter. The decanted wine loses part of the *bouquet* or its characteristic aroma, which is so much appreciated by connoisseurs.

In France, which is the first wine country in the world, nobody ever thinks of having wines decanted, as everybody is trained how to handle and serve them in the correct manner.

The reason for decanting wines in England may be safely attributed to the fact that unskilled waiters and untrained servants are apt to shake the bottles and so mix the sediment up with valuable old wines.

At the majority of *recherché* dinners, wines are decanted chiefly to decorate the table with rich cut-glass and silver-mounted decanters.

Fine wine tastes decidedly better when poured straight into the glasses from the original bottle, provided, of course, it is manipulated by a skilled butler with a steady hand.

All red wines, while in the bottles, throw down a certain amount of sediment.

When fine wines such as Burgundy, Claret, or old Port-wine are to be decanted, the bottles should be taken out of the bin held by the neck in the same horizontal position as they are in the bins, and carried steadily to the wire cradle or decanting basket placed on a firm table for the purpose. It is obvious to remark that this precaution is needed to avoid disturbing the sediment in the bottle and clouding the wine.

When these wines are colder than their proper temperature, the empty decanter should be immersed in warm water.

An electric light or a lighted candle must be on the table in readiness as a part of this operation.

A patent corkscrew is now required to open the bottle lying in the cradle. The uncorking of the bottle must be done in a scientific manner; carefully and gently, as the least jerk disturbs the sediment.

When the cork is drawn, wipe the mouth of the bottle gently, to prevent any particles of cork or dust from dropping into the decanter. Now, take the bottle by the middle with the right hand and hold in the left the warmed decanter (with a small bent silver-plated funnel placed in it). Pour the wine out gently against the light, carefully watching all the time the sediment, which can be plainly seen through the bottle held against the candle on the right-hand side of the operator.

When the sediment in the bottle reaches the neck, stop pouring at once; as none of the cloudy sediment must be allowed to go into the decanter. If the cork of the original bottle is not broken, place it loosely in the decanter; otherwise use the glass stopper.

The corks of old Port-wine bottles are, as a rule, perished or rotten, and can seldom be drawn whole; they come out in pieces, and generally cause trouble. When decanting Port-wine, a special nickel or silver-plated funnel with a double cup and double gauze between, should be used to make extra sure that no particles of any kind can get into the decanter.

Very old Port-wine bottles often have a thick crust round them which prevents one from seeing the contents of the bottle when decanting, in spite of having the light at the right side. This fact, therefore, involves extra precautions being taken to ensure obtaining a clear wine.

When a bottle of old Port-wine has its crust broken through undue shaking, the wine should be carefully strained and allowed to settle before serving.

Champagne, Hock, Moselle and similar wines are not as a rule decanted.

## HOW WINE AND MINERAL WATER BOTTLES SHOULD BE OPENED

There is really not much skill required in opening or uncorking a bottle of wine; yet there is hardly a restaurant-goer or a diner-out who cannot remember the clumsy waiter or the careless servant who once upon a time spoiled his garments with the contents of a bottle of Claret or Champagne.

For those who need guidance on this subject, the following instructions may be useful.

A lever or patent corkscrew is unquestionably the best to uncork either Claret or Port-wine.

The tops of the bottles of fine Claret, or Moselle and Rhine wine, generally have a tinfoil capsule or a metallic cap. Before uncorking one of these bottles, cut round the tinfoil half an inch from the top. Draw the cork carefully and wipe the mouth of the bottle with a special clean cloth. Now, pour out gently and take care never to fill the glasses up to the brim.

To uncork bottles of Champagne and mineral water, no greater difficulty should be experienced; only a little precaution and practice are required. Cut and remove the wire; then cut the string (if any) which is round the neck. Be careful not to allow the cork to escape from the hand. Hold the bottle by the neck with the right hand and grasp the cork with a cloth in the left. With a little twisting movement the cork will come out. See that the wine does not spurt and thus prevent accidents. Should the cork be a hard one and break, leaving half behind in the bottle, cut the cork off level and insert the patent corkscrew. By reversing this instrument the cork is soon drawn out.

Always wipe the mouth of the bottles properly before serving.

When Champagne is not at a very low temperature extra care must be taken to avoid accidents and losing the contents of the bottle.

Champagne and all stamped corks of vintage wines should be carefully wiped by the butler and placed on the table to the right (or left) side of the host. This is done *de rigueur* in all the best-class restaurants.

# CHAPTER 27

# EMPLOYER AND EMPLOYEE

## LEGAL POINTS INTERESTING
## BOTH TO MASTERS AND SERVANTS

The engagement of servants and hotel employees is often done in a very loose manner, and disputes not infrequently arise in consequence.

At the time of engagement a clear understanding should be come to as to the method of terminating the contract.

In some places, wages, although reckoned by the year, are usually paid quarterly, monthly, or weekly; in all three cases, a quarter's, a month's, or a week's notice (in some places only twenty-four hours') is commonly given when it is desired to dismiss either the servant or employee; or a quarter's, a month's, a week's, or twenty-four hours' wages may be given in lieu of notice, when it is desired to dismiss the employee on the spot.

There exist quite a number of firms adopting the system of not giving to, or requiring from, the employees any notice whatever; that is, they may leave the place or they may be dismissed at a moment's notice, without either side being entitled to any wages but those due at the time of leaving (these firms have, as a rule, a printed notice to that effect on the premises, and also on the application forms issued to and filled by the employees).

It is a common mistake to suppose that employees are entitled to either a month's or a week's board-wages in addition; such a demand cannot be enforced.

An employee may be instantly dismissed for drunkenness, immorality, dishonesty, gross impertinence, or refusal to do the lawful biddings of his or her master or mistress, or those representing them; and if when so dismissed the employee refuses to leave the premises, he or she may be ejected, reasonable force only being used.

An employee summarily dismissed is not entitled to any wages in lieu of notice, nor to any written references, but only to wages which have already become due at the time of dismissal.

An employee, or servant, can leave instantly (1) if he or she is improperly treated either by master, manager, or others representing them; (2) if he or she is abused or threatened, or in bodily fear; (3) if the food or lodgings is dangerous to health; (4) if the employee is legally justified in leaving, he or she is entitled to wages down to the time of leaving.

An employee is not, in law, liable for breakages, unless it can clearly be shown that these are from wilful carelessness or neglect.

An employer is not bound to provide medical attendance for any of his employees in case of illness; but if he sends for a medical man for the employee, he is liable, and cannot deduct expenses incurred from the employee's wages.

# CHAPTER 28

# THE BUTLER AND THE EFFICIENT MODERN WAITER

To efficiently fulfil the duties of butler in a private house, a thorough knowledge of waiting at table is most necessary; but owing to the fact that there are always the same number of people to be served, and the same routine to go through daily, any individual, however dull or new to the work, can soon get accustomed to the duties and become quite a model servant.

But this is not the case with respect to waiters in fashionable hotels or restaurants. To be a perfectly efficient waiter, as is everywhere requisite nowadays, is not so easy as it may appear at first sight; and although there are still many people who think that a waiter need know nothing more than to hand and carry dishes backwards and forwards from the table, such is not by any means the case in reality.

With the exception of the club waiter, the majority of the number of English waiters that have existed up to the outbreak of the war have been employed chiefly at second-rate hotels or serving teas at various exhibition grounds, and are (or were) men who took up waiting not as a legitimate trade, but as a last resource, when everything else had failed them. They have (or had) no proper training or idea of what is expected from them.

Circumstances, however, have altered matters, and it is time that 'Robert' should now turn over a new leaf, and fit himself for the requirements of up-to-date establishments.

I propose to point out in this chapter some of the perfect waiter's equipments, and how to begin to acquire the necessary accomplishments.

A young waiter wishing to become competent in his profession must first of all serve several years' apprenticeship, and then travel in order to learn various languages (firstly French), and also to study foreign customs; as the Hotel and Restaurant industry is of a cosmopolitan character.

As a matter of fact, all the foreign waiters who hold good positions at first-class establishments at the present moment are accomplished linguists.

During his apprenticeship he must cultivate and develop many good qualities. An authority once said that 'to be a waiter, it is necessary to possess the manners and tact of a diplomat, the elegance of a young duke, the wisdom of Solomon, and the patience of Job.'

He certainly must be immaculately clean in his appearance and in his method of working; must be nimble as a squirrel, diligent, discreet, attentive and obsequious towards his customers, and obedient and respectful towards his superiors.

This may seem greatly exaggerated, but it is perfectly true; and unless the future waiter acquires these qualities, there is not much chance of his rising in his profession, or becoming one day a good Maître d'hôtel or Manager of a first-class establishment.

Besides the above qualities, he must be little short of an actor, since he has to learn perfect self-control and the power of moulding himself to circumstances; and though he often has to call upon his reserve store of patience, and sometimes could justly feel anger or dissatisfaction, he could not commit a greater error than show it to his superiors, under pain of losing his situation.

Before thinking of filling the position of a responsible waiter, such as the taking charge of a 'rang' or station in a *restaurant de luxe* with service *à la grande carte*, he must work for some time as *commis* or waiter's assistant, in order to become acquainted with an infinity of preliminaries which it is absolutely essential to know for the position.

After passing through the rudimentary stage of learning to wash glasses, clean silver, etc., he must learn how to read the menu; that is, to understand the exact meaning of the French culinary technical terms; for these terms explain in themselves the composition of the dishes and how they are cooked and served.

At all first-class establishments, the menus are always written in French; and they are often irksome—nay, enigmas—even to epicures with a thorough knowledge of French, as these technical expressions form a special language of their own.

A well-trained waiter who can read the menu is thus able to explain the composition of any particular dish or dishes on the menu or on *la carte du jour*, if any of his customers ask him to do so. Besides he is enabled to offer or to propose any delicacy on the bill of fare, and to order same from the chef with the certainty of accurate knowledge.

Besides this, he must know how to manipulate and serve all table-wines, at their exact temperature, and with the dishes they should accompany.

He is also expected to know how to carve every kind of fish, meat and bird, how to prepare and properly mix salads, how to make tea, coffee, cocoa, etc., and, on special occasions, if necessary, to show skill in decorating the table artistically with choice flowers.

With regard to long or short drinks, he is expected to know how to prepare and serve champagne or claret cups, cocktails or any other beverage.

Although, as I have said before, the above may be considered to be exaggeration, I repeat that it is not so, and that a waiter nowadays is in no wise considered proficient to occupy a post in a first-class establishment, unless he possesses all the above accomplishments.

The public of to-day, that is, the hotel and restaurant goers, are becoming each time more and more exacting; some customers even think a waiter is a living encyclopædia of general knowledge, and will ask him such things as the probable winner for the Derby, the score in the Test matches, what plays are at the various theatres, or when the *Aquitania* sails for America.

The late Mr. Carl Ritz, the recognised *Roi des Hôteliers* and pioneer of the luxurious Hotels bearing his name all over the world, once said that 'every Hotel and Restaurant employee

147

should always bear in mind the words, *Le client a toujours raison* (the customer is always right).

The waiter's motto for all his customers should be *Ich Dien*.

CHAPTER 29

# THE MAÎTRE D'HÔTEL

As explained in the previous chapter, a perfect or carefully trained waiter is one who is an adept in Hot-plate drill, Table-laying, and serving dinners generally; but this is only the A.B.C. or the rudiments of the business.

If in the course of his many years' practice of these rudiments he manages to acquire the manners of an ambassador, the palate of a *cordon-bleu*, the wine knowledge of an expert wine-dealer, the cheerfulness and the graces of a society hostess, and the long-suffering endurance of both Ulysses and Job, for bores, wealthy maniacs, fribbles, Hotel-cranks and Restaurant-faddists, he is then (only then) ripe to become Maître d'hôtel.

The rôle of the Maître d'hôtel in large establishments is to-day quite different to what it used to be fifteen or twenty years ago;

especially on the Continent, where the hotels and restaurants generally belonged to a single proprietor. Mine host used to be then a caterer of practical experience himself, and the Maître d'hôtel was his right hand and confidential man.

The modern large establishments of to-day belong mostly to public companies, and, as a rule, those on the Board of Management know little or nothing as to how a modern hotel should be conducted. They leave everything in the hands of the manager, and he in turn to the heads of the different departments.

A truly accomplished Maître d'hôtel is a real artist and quite indispensable in the dining-room and restaurant of these establishments.

Possibly, patrons of the higher arts will tilt their noses superciliously when they read this assertion; but, because a man cannot compose an opera, or paint for the Royal Academy, is he any the less an artist in other respects?

An educated and experienced waiter is as much a trained product as a graduate of a technical school, or a modern medical practitioner. His every move is the result of a careful study. The very stoop of his shoulders, the length of his stride, his countenance, are all the result of long years of practice.

The graceful and dignified manner in which he receives the patrons of the establishment, and the tact he shows in proposing just what they want, cannot be acquired in an hour.

His accomplishments also do not end with the mere knack of reaching a climax of perfection in that respect. The genuine Maître d'hôtel is a past-master in the art of fancy cooking, and can equally hand a chafing-dish and make the sauce for a pressed wild duck at a gourmet's table, as to prepare a delicious iced fruit *macédoine.*

He is also a connoisseur regarding all the little 'fillers-in' which help to make a repast a delight to the epicure. What he does not know about the prime cuts is not worth chronicling; and when it comes to wines, cocktails, or cooling cups, he is equally excellent.

When a diner-out is in doubt about what goes best with this or that dish, he is just as ready to give his counsel; whilst the manner in which he carves a bird at the epicure's table is something worth watching. The departed Joseph at the Savoy Restaurant had the carving skill of Kubelik's fiddling.

He is a thorough expert at ordering a dinner from the *Hors-d'œuvre* down to the *café*. And what a consolation and guide he is to the lonely diner-out or the crabbed old gentleman, tired of himself and everything else, who sinks down into a chair and asks this obsequious man at his side to pick him out 'a good dinner that tastes like something.'

He knows at a glance what sort of *mets* will appeal to the *blasé* palate of his customer, and what wine will go best with the dishes he selects and orders.

He is sure to have a few original recipes with which to tempt his patron's appetite, and he is the inventor of more than a few salad dressings for which he has been many times complimented.

Likewise, he is a good judge of cigars; and when he is asked for a 'medium strong Habana' he knows just the cigar required; for 'medium strong' does not mean 'medium', nor does 'strong', and he sees that the patron gets what he wants.

He requires to be a good organiser and strict disciplinarian, to keep his waiters under him well posted and drilled, so as to carry out his instructions automatically, and to serve the patrons skilfully and in the most courteous manner.

There is a rare quality possessed by the expert Maître d'hôtel which is seldom noticed or appreciated by the management of the establishment. I mean that peculiar courtesy and far-reaching diplomacy that characterise him. Supposing a patron with very fastidious tastes ordered of him a grouse or a partridge roasted 'medium', and though he was careful enough to underline 'medium' on the kitchen-check, it was sent to the table too well done; the Maître d'hôtel will know by the expression of the customer's face that he is displeased, and will immediately set about putting things right.

This is where he shows diplomatic traits from which more than one ambassador could take a few points.

There are two ends which the Maître d'hôtel diplomat must attain because of the fault of a careless cook. First, he must avoid, if possible, the return of the bird to the kitchen, which always means a breach of friendly relations between the restaurant staff and the dictator of the range; to say nothing of the partial loss to the establishment.

Secondly, he must at the same time smooth the ruffled feelings of the guest, so that he eats the overdone bird and likes it.

Of course, the Maître d'hôtel insists that the bird in question be returned to the kitchen and another one more underdone be cooked and served; but he insists in such a pleasing, apologetic, almost tearful manner, that the guest has not the heart to acquiesce.

Throughout the rest of the meal he is the apogee of consideration; he is ever hovering at the guest's side, anticipating his every wish, suggesting a little entrée here, bringing a nice salad there, paying all sorts of attentions with such a correct deportment, that finally the guest says to himself 'that wasn't such a bad dinner after all.'

For the lonely diner-out, a stray unit in a large city like London, the Maître d'hôtel is a godsend to be able to talk to on cognate subjects and, if necessary, in various languages.

CHAPTER 30

# THE POURBOIRE
# OR 'TIPPING' SYSTEM

There are few subjects which have, I think, been so often and so warmly discussed in the Hotel and Restaurant world for the last few years as the *pourboire* or 'tipping' system.

This question seems also to appeal vividly to the public or restaurant-goers, judging by the numerous letters they send from time to time to the Press, the large amount of interest they create, and the heated manner in which they discuss the 'tip' or little *douceur* which is given to the attentive waiter.

Many of the letters published during the last crusade were from people who have a great aversion to the 'tipping' custom; in fact, they call it a gross imposition, and suggest that the hotel and restaurant employees ought to be placed on the same footing as the employees of other trades who do not and ought not to expect anything else besides the price of the goods they sell.

Acting on these sentiments, several catering firms have instituted various establishments, which are known as 'non-gratuity' places, with the intention of securing the patronage of those people possessing the 'tipping' aversion.

Whether those places have been, or are, actually successful solely because they are conducted on the 'non-tip' principle is quite problematical. One thing is quite certain: the 'tipping' question has always been most unsavoury to all people concerned, *i.e.*, the givers and receivers of tips in general, and this in spite of what some people may say to the contrary.

As everybody knows, there is a large number of hotel and restaurant goers, who, through circumstances, are obliged to patronise the fashionable establishments; but, being possessed of very small means, are compelled to study the strictest economy. These people are naturally unable to give any *pourboire*, or to comply with the tipping custom, and hence find the principle an abomination. It is not surprising, therefore, if these people advocate the abolition of such a 'hideous system', as they call it.

On the other hand, a self-respecting man who, through circumstances of life, is obliged to earn his living waiting on the patrons of these establishments also detests the idea of being dependent for his living on the fanciful inclination of this public.

Now, employees and workers of all trades and professions are paid so much per hour or per week, according to their merits. Why are not the waiters paid similarly? Waiting in a modern establishment requires no mean ability on the part of the waiter. Why should he be treated or paid differently to a skilful labourer?

Cannot the hotel proprietors see their way to pay their employees a living wage, or about the same amount they generally get, both with the gratuities and the present meagre wages they actually receive? They could easily raise their prices from 10 to 20 per cent., and if all the caterers by mutual consent adopted this system, the whole vexatious question could be ended.

Hotel proprietors and managers know very well that the majority of their visitors prefer to know in advance the amount they will have to pay for their food and accommodation, so as to know how much they can spend on their wines and other extras. Also they know that the majority of them hate the idea of having to 'tip' on their departure, from the Hall-porter and Head waiter down to the pageboy of the place.

The great majority of hotel and restaurant customers, and this could easily be stretched to liner passengers, do 'tip' the employees unwillingly. They condescend to do so, for various reasons; some because, having received all kinds of attentions and civility during a certain period from the servants, they are afraid to incur black looks on their departure, knowing well these servants are not adequately paid by the management, and they expect something from them. Others, intending to return to the same establishment on a future date, fear to be received or attended by these same servants in a quite different spirit.

Those visitors who cannot afford to give 'tips', or are mean, and do not care what the hotel (or boat) servants may think or say behind their backs, either dodge the employees on their departure, or do what is a common occurrence; they create a disturbance or make an imaginary complaint against the servants at the last moment, so as to be justified, apparently, for leaving the hotel without giving any gratuities.

These people, as a rule, never return to the same establishment, thus constituting a disquieting question even for the management.

As it will be seen, the tipping system is undesirable by all parties concerned and ought to be abolished by Act of Parliament.

But there are still many people, both hotel patrons and servants, who prefer and advocate the 'tipping' system, and these present another side to this question.

Everybody knows that it makes all the difference in the world to hotel and restaurant diners or guests when their table is tastefully laid out and their dinner properly served; and a waiter serving dinner to hotel visitors in their own apartments, or in a restaurant, can easily mar or make the meal a delight, by the way he serves it.

The verb 'to wait', according to the definition in my dictionary, is 'to stay for, or to remain stationary in expectation of the arrival of some one, for an indefinite period.' Now, the waiter who does not expect any *douceur* whatever for his diligent services and his painstakings has it entirely in his own hands to make the diners 'do' that.

It is to prevent being kept waiting for an indefinite period, etc., that the tip was invented.

The word 'TIP' does not mean in this particular case the top or end of anything, but 'To-Insure-Promptitude' from the person who serves.

The average hotel visitor or restaurant-goer who is in the happy position of giving tips does not like to give less than the usual amount, as he dislikes the idea of being regarded by the employees as mean.

At first-class restaurants, wealthy customers never leave on the plate less than 1*s*. per head after the dinner or supper bill has been paid. At breakfast or luncheon time, this is generally halved; 6*d*. per head being considered an ample tip.

Wealthy *habitués*, who often seek the Maître d'hôtel's advice on matters of their special dinner-parties, never forget to put something in his hand.

At these places all tips are put in the 'Tronc' and are daily counted and entered in the tronc-book; every waiter, as well as the Maître d'hôtel, having a column allocated to him. The total amount is divided at the end of every week according to the length of service in the establishment and the ability and position of each individual.

Visitors staying at hotels with their families give to the waiter 1*s*. per person per day; that is, for serving three or four meals, and this is reckoned a proper average.

Of course, the question of tips is more or less an affair of purse and generosity on the part of the tip-giver. Some have much of one but little of the other and vice-versa.

At second-rate hotels and restaurants, the average tip given to waiters is about half the amount mentioned above.

I wish to make it quite clear that the charge for attendance which appears on the hotel bills does *not* go into the employee's pockets, as some visitors imagine. On the contrary; should a waiter forget or omit to charge on the bill, say, for a bottle of wine, or any other item partaken of by a visitor, the waiter is made to pay for same out of his scanty wages.

I would also like to mention here the unfair conditions under which waiters work in some places (which I have on several occasions exposed in the Press).

I mean those restaurants where waiters receive no wages whatever, and out of their tips they are made to pay for the newspapers, tooth-picks and matches used by the customers, as well as for the breakages. At some other restaurants the waiters have even to pay a few shillings daily to the proprietor for the privilege of working in the place.

In conclusion, in spite of the discussions and controversies that have appeared from time to time in the Press, nothing definite has been arrived at yet as to whether the 'tipping' system should be encouraged or discontinued. There are still many people who prefer to keep the old custom of 'tipping' their waiter, maintaining that really good service cannot be obtained otherwise; and that not only waiters, but Railway porters, Taxi-drivers, Hairdressers and numbers of others expect to be 'tipped' if they are to give their best services.